SUCCESS STORIES

How
eleven
of Japan's
most interesting
businesses
came
to be

SUCCESS STORIES

How
eleven
of Japan's
most interesting
businesses
came
to be

Direction by Leonard Koren
Coordination by Peter Goodman
Illustration by Shack Mihara
Research by Ziggie Y. Kato & Shinichi Sudo

Chronicle Books • San Francisco

Printed in Japan

Library of Congress Cataloging-in-Pubication Data

Koren, Leonard.
Success stories: how eleven of Japan's most interesting businessses came to be/by Leonard Koren: illustrated by Shack Mihara.
p. cm.
ISBN 0-87701-635-6
1. Business enterprises—Japan—Case studies.
2. Success in business—Japan—Case studies.
I. Mihara, Shack. II. Title.
HF5349.J3K67 1990
338.7'4'0952—dc20
89-48253
CIP

Distributed in Canada by
Raincoast Books
112 East Third Avenue
Vancouver, B.C.
V5T 1C8

10 9 8 7 6 5 4 3 2 1

Chronicle Books
275 Fifth Street
San Francisco, California 94103

Note: (1) In this book, the names of Japanese active before the mid-19th century appear in Japanese order, with the family name preceding the given name. Names of modern Japanese appear in Western order, with the given name first. (2) Wherever appropriate, modern dollar equivalents have been given for yen amounts at the approximate rate of US$1 = ¥140. Currency fluctuations over the years have made it impossible to convert all yen amounts.

CONTENTS

From earliest times, myths have served not only to explain the world as we see it, but also to inspire us in our own quests. In this book are eleven Japanese business success stories retold in mythic form. Bold illustrations and brief text sketches are used to isolate the essential, inspirational core. These stories were selected for a variety of reasons. Dentsu, Matsushita Electric, and Shiseido were chosen because they are powerful enterprises that exert a pervasive influence on everyday Japanese life. Nissin Foods and Mujirushi Ryohin are here because they epitomize the Japanese genius for clever packaging and skillful marketing. Urasenke and Mitsui are good examples of very old businesses organized around uniquely Japanese formulas. Tokyo Disneyland, in contrast, represents one of the few business sectors for which the Japanese still need foreign assistance—high-concept entertainment venues. Mori Building is here because it is an anomaly: a conscionable player in the spectacular Tokyo real estate game. Finally, the Folio agency and Fox Bagels represent the growing number of small, entrepreneurial enterprises in Japan (and because the owner of one of them is an American, they also show it *can* be done).

Some quick observations about what these stories teach us. First, the mythical Japanese businessman is no indomitable giant. He is rather more like us, and even in consensus-oriented Japan the determination and personal vision of the company founder are crucial to the success of the company. Second, it helps to be Japanese and to have rich and powerful connections—but these aren't necessary. Third, Japan really *is* different. Fourth, there are rich rewards for those who succeed there.

For those more interested in history, the Appendix provides interpretive comments, incidental details, and background information. Note the extent to which America looms large within the Japanese mythology. In one way or another, most modern Japanese companies owe a debt to America. America provided corporate and manufacturing models. It provided aid, orders for industry, and a huge consumer market after World War II. More important, America has long been the dream inspiration for Japanese visionaries, style makers, and entrepreneurs. Perhaps this book's depictions of strategies and tactics for making it in Japan will become part of the still-emerging American dream.

MATSUSHITA ELECTRIC

Japan's
Horatio Alger story
and a world leader
in consumer electronics

Konosuke Matsushita was born in 1894 in the village of Wasamura, south of Kyoto. His father, a farmer, owned a small amount of land but did little farming himself. When the Russo-Japanese War ended, Konosuke's father lost all the family property in the frenzied commodity markets. The Matsushitas sold everything and with the help of a friend opened a wooden clog shop, which soon failed. Then the three oldest children died of influenza. Konosuke was the last surviving son, and at age nine was sent to Osaka, where he became an apprentice at a hibachi shop and later at a shop that made and sold bicycles.

The founder, one of the world's great industrialists, is born the son of a farmer and the youngest of eight children.

Konosuke was happy at the bicycle shop, but believing that the future lay with electricity, he quit to obtain a job at the Osaka Electric Light Company as an interior wiring assistant. He was fifteen. Three years later he married Mumeno Iue. At Osaka Electric he was promoted to inspector and began to experiment with a design for a new light socket. Konosuke had a secure position, but he was restless, and at age twenty-one he left the company to develop his light socket. He set up shop with two ex–Osaka Electric employees and with his wife's younger brother, Toshio Iue, who would later found the Sanyo Electric Company.

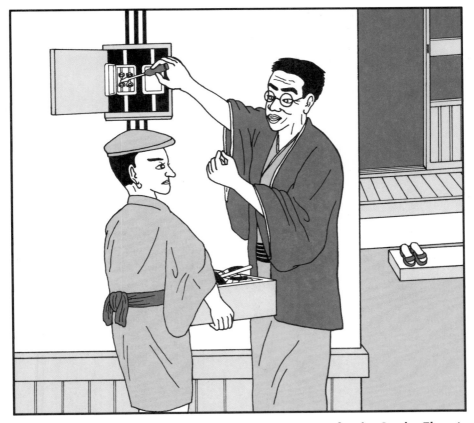

Konosuke goes to work as an interior wiring assistant for the Osaka Electric Light Company.

The fledgling enterprise worked out of two rooms in a tenement in eastern Osaka. Konosuke and his wife slept in one corner of the smaller room. The four business partners had only ¥100 (about $100 at the time), and not one of them knew how to manufacture or price a light socket. The big problem was figuring out how to make the insulation. Konosuke analyzed fragments of discarded insulation at a local factory, but that didn't help. Finally he learned the formula from an ex–Osaka Electric employee who had gone to work for an insulation manufacturer and then failed when he tried to start his own business.

In a small tenement apartment, Konosuke and his partners try to figure out how to make a light socket.

It was 1917. After ten months the partners had managed to sell only 100 sockets for a profit of ¥10. All except Konosuke and his wife's brother, Toshio, went back to their regular jobs. In December, just when they had almost given up on improving their socket design, an electrical parts wholesaler approached them with an order for 1,000 electric fan insulation plates to be used by Kawakita Electric Company. If the quality was good, Kawakita would probably take 30,000 plates a year. The initial order was due the end of the month. The plates were easy to make, so Konosuke decided to give up on his light socket for the time being.

Konosuke makes no money at first. His wife has to pawn her clothing to keep the family going.

Kawakita liked Konosuke's insulators and placed new orders. In the spring the factory moved to a larger house and began producing an attachment plug from recycled used light sockets. It was a cheap but quality product. Unable to keep up with the demand, Konosuke had a new factory built. He had thirty employees and was rapidly developing new products (a two-way light socket) and new markets (Tokyo, Nagoya, Kyushu). Instead of keeping his manufacturing secrets "in the family," like other electrical companies, Konosuke taught even his newest employees all the tricks of the trade. He trusted them.

After receiving an order for more insulation plates, Konosuke moves his operation to a larger house.

In 1923 Konosuke turned his attention to bike lamps. Existing lamps used either candles or short-lived batteries. Konosuke's new lamp used a better bulb and battery that lasted thirty to fifty hours. But no distributor or bike shop believed it could be that good. So Konosuke delivered free lamps to retail stores all over Osaka. Turning one on, he would say, "Watch how long before it burns out, and then sell the others only when you're sure the customer will be satisfied. If you don't like the lamp, you owe us nothing." The scheme worked, and Konosuke soon had distributors calling in orders.

After meeting extreme resistance to his battery-powered bicycle lamp, Konosuke develops a novel marketing scheme.

The company was now the Matsushita Electric Works. It had 300 employees and monthly sales over ¥100,000. When the 1929 depression hit, business fell off. The company had borrowed money, couldn't sell its products, and was threatened with bankruptcy. Konosuke, always sickly, fell gravely ill and had to leave Osaka to convalesce. Two managers came to his sickbed and said they could save the company if half the employees were fired. Konosuke disagreed. Instead, he said, halve production and continue at full pay but with no holidays, and then get all the employees to help move unsold merchandise. This enlightened plan worked, and in a few months the company was back to full-time production.

Even when ill, Konosuke lives and breathes business and comes up with enlightened management ideas.

In 1937 there were nine companies in the Matsushita group. War fever was growing in Japan. Foreign trade and banking were restricted by the military. Then the government began directing companies to shift their production to the manufacture of munitions. Konosuke had to stop making fan and room heaters—"luxury items." His production of radios, light bulbs, and batteries was curtailed. To remain in business, he made guns, bayonets, propellers, and even wooden ships and wooden planes. By 1945 many of Konosuke's factories were under the direct control of the military.

Immediately before and during World War II, the company is directed to switch production to military applications.

Japan was defeated. General MacArthur ordered that all military-controlled factories be shut down. He set out to break up the zaibatsu, the large industrial enterprise groups that had financed the war effort. Matsushita, despite its small size (sixty related companies) was on the hit list. Konosuke was told to resign. He compiled 5,000 pages of reports in his favor and petitioned against the order. In the end, it was union leaders who persuaded the Americans to let Konosuke stay. But his personal assets were frozen, and the companies he owned had enormous debts. The press dubbed Konosuke "Japan's King of Arrearage." In mid-1950 he and his companies were at last allowed to return to normal production.

After the war, Konosuke is almost purged from his position by the anti-zaibatsu regulations of the American Occupation.

Konosuke was determined to rebuild and reevaluate his methods from a global perspective. In January 1951 he left for America, intending to stay one month. He stayed three. He was amazed at how rich America was. A standard General Electric radio sold for $24 in a department store. An American worker, who earned $1.50 an hour, could buy it with two days' labor. To buy a Matsushita Electric radio that cost ¥9,000 would take a Japanese worker a month and a half of wages. New York City's power consumption was equal to that of all of Japan. Konosuke saw a movie a day and determined he would be as successful as the Americans.

On his first trip to America, Konosuke begins parting his hair on the side and has his eyes opened to international opportunities.

In July 1952 Konosuke began negotiations with the Dutch company Philips about forming a technological tie-up to produce electronics parts in Japan. Philips wanted $500,000, 30% of the stock in the new company, and a 6% technical guidance fee. Konosuke balked at the 6% fee. He said that since his company would be managing the joint venture, it should get a management fee. Philips rejected the idea as absurd. But the Japanese stubbornness impressed the Dutch. In October the deal was signed, giving Philips a 4.5% technical guidance fee and Matsushita a 3% management fee. In 1954 the new company began producing vacuum tubes, transistors, and other components.

Negotiations are tough, but Konosuke is able to sign a technical licensing agreement with a Dutch electronics company.

Konosuke retired from Matsushita Electric in 1973 but he continued to speak out on the issues that interested him. He proposed that Japan create more space for housing and farming by leveling off 20% of its land and using the removed earth to extend the shoreline or create new islands. The PHP Institute ("Peace and Happiness through Prosperity") he established is devoted to studying the problems of humankind. The Matsushita School of Government and Business offers a program for training a new generation of leaders. "I am proud to say that I have done my very best each day."

Before his death in 1989, a retired Konosuke, living in a Matsushita-built hospital, maintains a high profile as a visionary thinker.

MITSUI GROUP

A nearly
400-year-old
business giant
is a player
in every sector of
the Japanese economy

Civil wars raged constantly in medieval Japan. The Mitsui family served as retainers to a feudal lord in Omi Province, strategically located between Nagoya and the imperial capital of Kyoto. Although of samurai (warrior) rank, the Mitsui were primarily clerk/bureaucrats. In 1568 the army of rival warlord Nobunaga decimated Omi Province on its way to imperial Kyoto. His castle destroyed, Takayasu, head of the Mitsui household, fled with his family to the safe haven of Matsusaka to the east, near the holy Ise Shrine. After Nobunaga's death, Tokugawa Ieyasu emerged as the ruler of Japan in 1603 and based his government in Edo, present-day Tokyo.

The now-masterless Takayasu, head of the Mitsui family, realizes that maybe there is more to life than being a samurai.

From pilgrims to Ise, Takayasu's son Sokubei heard of the growth of commerce under Ieyasu now that the country was at peace. On his journeys to Edo he saw how the samurai, in need of weaponry and supplies, had fallen into debt at the hands of the merchants, who were by far their social inferiors. Sokubei decided that, although of warrior class, he could best repair the ill fortune of his family by renouncing his rank and going into business. With the civil wars over and a money economy emerging, one could now make a secure living in an honest trade.

Hearing that commerce is booming in Edo, Takayasu's son decides to trade his samurai sword for a merchant's abacus.

Sokubei opened up a brewery that made sake and soy sauce. The ex-samurai proved inept at business, but his wife, Shuho, the daughter of a merchant, took charge and expanded into pawnbroking and money lending. The shop thrived as its clientele drank themselves foolish and parted with more and more of their money. Always thrifty and hard-working, Shuho encouraged these same traits in eight sons and daughters. In time she sent her first son, Saburozaemon, off to Edo to open a draper's shop called Echigoya. Her youngest son, Hachirobei, soon joined him there.

Sokubei is more adept at the courtly arts of his aristocratic heritage and leaves the running of the business to his wife.

Hachirobei learned a great deal at Echigoya in bustling Edo, but after fourteen years had to return home to help his now elderly mother. Back in Matsusaka, he mastered the art of managing capital and making money on floats and interest. He financed farmers and took their land as collateral. He became an expert on rice commodity trading. And he learned to be wary of samurai lords, who paid infrequently and sometimes not at all. Hachirobei married and had six sons. At age fifty-one he began a fabric wholesale business in Kyoto and then a new Echigoya shop in Edo.

Hachirobei displays a natural talent for business and develops into a virtuoso moneylender serving farmers and samurai lords.

Hachirobei devoted himself to doing business with the more reliable commoners in Edo and revolutionized Japanese business practices. He sold cloth in any length, not just kimono sizes. He charged low prices and made money on volume. Most important, he sold on a cash-and-carry basis, with no bartering. Other merchants resented his success, but soon emulated his new methods. Hachirobei moved his store to a new site in Nihonbashi, where it became a major tourist attraction. He treated his clerks well, developed double-entry bookkeeping, and made a great deal of money.

Hachirobei's Edo shop is a sensation among shoppers and sightseers. On rainy days courtesy umbrellas festoon the streets with free advertisement.

Hachirobei wangled a posting as official purveyor of fabric to the government. He then created a lucrative national network of money changers, spawning a financial empire built on interest, currency, and commodities. Before he died in 1694 he made another innovation: instead of giving his estate to his elder son, he split it up among his children to effectively create a corporate "family." At the head was his eldest son, Takahira. Takahira, before his own death, drafted a constitution that was the inspiration of the Mitsui family until World War II. Among its admonitions: always be frugal and strive for political favor.

The family wisdom is passed down in the form of a document urging prudence, frugality, and, above all, strength through togetherness.

Civil war returned to Japan in the mid-19th century. As leading financiers, the Mitsui were called upon by the government to fund its assault on the rebel forces. But the Mitsui, with little money left in their coffers, were wary of getting involved. In stepped Rihachi Minogawa in 1866, a lowborn confectioner who was a longtime friend of the commissioner of finance. Rihachi agreed to intercede to protect the Mitsui from government demands. In return, he demanded that the Mitsui group be split up and that he himself—an outsider—be placed in charge of the branch that dealt with all government business.

Rihachi Minogawa, born an impoverished nobody, tells the Mitsui family heads how he will rescue their empire—for a price.

Both the government and the rebels—who supported a return to imperial rule—needed funds for their campaigns. The Mitsui were expected to guarantee the government's issue of paper money. At the same time they also controlled much of the funds used by the anti-government forces. Finally forced to choose sides, the Mitsui threw their support to the rebels, who were clearly winning anyway. A Mitsui was asked to become exchange agent to the victorious imperial government and graciously accepted with a gift of 1,000 gold coins to the court officials.

The Mitsui find ways of supporting each side in the battle for political control, thus assuring their position no matter what the outcome.

The Mitsui were crucial to the new government's program of modern industrialization. The government would pay for Western expertise and machinery and then turn the fledgling industry over to companies like Mitsui to run. A paper mill, numerous textile factories (including silk and cotton), a machine works (which would evolve into today's Toshiba), and the company that installed Tokyo's first electric lights in 1883 were all operated or funded by Mitsui, with the government's support.

In 1872 the new government sets up a modern silk-reeling mill, which the Mitsui use to help create Japan's textile industry.

A Mitsui branch founded to handle foreign commerce and shipping developed in 1876 into Mitsui Bussan, today one of the world's largest trading companies. Coal was its mainstay, but it also owned sources of lead, zinc, iron, and (as an inflation hedge) gold. It had its own steamship line and supplied half of all machinery imported into Japan. In the 1890s, under the leadership of another outsider, Hikojiro Nakamigawa, Mitsui reorganized its disparate divisions—bank, trading company, and mining—into a single entity, the Mitsui Partnership Bank.

A coal mine run by a Japanese graduate of MIT exploits its workers but gets the job done with the latest Western equipment.

Japan chafed under the unequal treaties imposed on it by foreign powers. In the 1890s it became a colonial power itself. Through its war with China, it acquired Taiwan and a huge war indemnity. Behind the scenes were the Mitsui. Their factories received orders and government subsidies. They supplied war materials to the front. They handled the money that paid the armed forces. Their mines supplied fuel. The ex-samurai rulers of Japan, who had bestowed titles of nobility on themselves in 1884, rewarded Hachiroemon Takaaki, ninth head of the family, by making him Baron Mitsui.

BARON – MITSUI Hachiroemon Takaaki

In return for his work during the Sino-Japanese War, the head of Mitsui is made a baron and enters the inner sanctum of official power.

In the 1920s Japan relied on exports to earn money to buy raw materials. When the crash came, Japan found itself blocked from foreign markets by protective tariffs. It fought back by lowering its prices almost beyond reason. It slashed wages at home and retooled its factories. It cut back on quality and materials. As a result, the British weaving industry was destroyed, and racist passions flared in the U.S. Gaining control of plantations, raw materials, and manufacturing venues throughout the world, and handling the bulk of Japan's exports at this time, was Mitsui Bussan.

During the Great Depression, the Japanese—through Mitsui—flood world markets with cheap goods, destroying overseas industries.

By the 1930s Mitsui had control of 15% of Japan's financial capital. To protect its interests, Mitsui (along with other enterprise groups, or zaibatsu, like Sumitomo) resisted any moves by labor to organize or by government to nationalize and thus restrict profit. The Mitsui had allies in the wartime cabinet and supplied most of the lead for the army's bullets. Mitsui was given virtual control of the exploitation of resources in China and Manchuria, and forced Koreans and Chinese to work themselves to death in its mines.

The Japanese annex Manchuria in 1932. In the following years, Mitsui profits mightily from munitions, resources, and conscript labor.

Mitsui, which before the war had traded with the British and Americans, expected business as usual after the surrender. It planned to move into housing construction and rice production. The Americans, however, wanted to bust up Mitsui and the other war-profiteering zaibatsu to promote more democratic market forces. The zaibatsu protested their innocence, but no one believed them, particularly as their role in China became known and as their secret hoards of precious wartime commodities were found. Mitsui, in October 1945, was forced to dissolve.

Mitsui leaders are surprised to hear that the Americans intend to break up the zaibatsu as punishment for their role in the war.

The Americans disagreed on how to deal with Japan. Reformers wanted American-style democracy, while hawks wanted to rebuild Japan to fight communism. Many of the Japanese who ran the government and dealt with the Americans were Mitsui men in one way or another, through marriage, school, or business connections. As insiders they were privy to Occupation plans, and if they couldn't head off the dissolution of the zaibatsu they could at least stall it. In the end, however, the Mitsui had to give up almost everything. As the richest of all, they had the most to lose.

The deposed Mitsui leaders, kept apprised of squabbles among the Americans, try to manipulate them behind the scenes.

In 1949 the Occupation authorities announced that the concentration of big business in Japan had been broken. But this was only apparently true, for the Japanese zaibatsu groups had maneuvered the Americans to water down many of the proposed restrictions on their activities. In place of the large holding companies like Mitsui emerged the old zaibatsu banks as the new linchpins of control. The banks provided loans to the former members of the group and, when the holding companies' stock was sold off, also became shareholders in many of Japan's leading corporations.

Trying to salvage what they can, the zaibatsu hire lobbyists and enlist many Americans to their aid, among them Richard Nixon.

Some of the fuel for Japanese industrial development after the war came from American investors. Daiichi Bussan, for example, a descendant of zaibatsu Mitsui Bussan trading company, was kept afloat by a loan of $140,000 from Chemical Bank and the Bache and Company brokerage. Many American corporations, too, who had been large stockholders in Japanese zaibatsu enterprises before the war, helped these companies rebuild after the war with money, technological assistance, and marketing aid. General Electric helped rebuild Toshiba. Westinghouse aided Mitsubishi Electric.

Yasutaro Niizeki, head of a Mitsui-descended trading company, flies to New York to persuade the Americans to loan him money.

Cold War hysteria in the early 1950s led the Americans to shore up Japan as a bulwark against communism. With the Korean War raging (and the American forces in need of supplies), this had to be done quickly—and who was more qualified to lead Japan back into the ranks of industrialization and militarism than the once-deposed zaibatsu leaders? Many of the Occupation reforms were moderated, and remnants of the huge prewar business empires recombined. Leftist opposition was stamped out, a "Self-Defense Force" was created, and the postwar outline of Japan Inc. emerged.

We're having a little problem in Korea. We'd like your help. You're now officially depurged... And you can have your factories back.

The Korean War begins. The Americans decide that a strong, anticommunist ally is better than a too-liberal Western-style democracy.

Of fifty-three Mitsui companies in 1945, a dozen disappeared completely and a few were broken up, but the rest emerged almost intact in the 1950s as the Mitsui Group. At the center was the Mitsui Bank. The various Mitsui companies all hold shares in each other's enterprises, creating a vast web of mutual control very different from the pyramidal power structure of prewar business. The way Mitsui Aluminum was formed in 1969 is a good example of how the group operates. (1) Mitsui executives, who socialize regularly, come up with the idea of using surplus coal to generate electricity to make much-needed aluminum. (2, 3) A committee decides the plant will be at Omuta, where Mitsui has

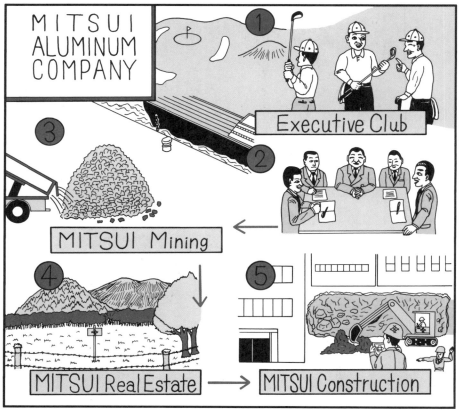

Mitsui comes roaring back. Today it is a huge enterprise capable of mining, manufacturing, and selling just about any commodity . . .

coal mines and shipping facilities. (4, 5) The site is developed by Mitsui companies. (6) The trading company branch acquires technology and equipment. (7, 8) Mitsui companies together create a new company in Australia to mine and process bauxite, which is shipped to Japan on Mitsui freighters. (9) The docks and plant are a joint project of other Mitsui companies. (10) Managing financing for the whole deal is Mitsui Bank. (11) The trading company returns to promote sales, including sales to members of the Mitsui group who, having invested in the scheme, will now profit from it.

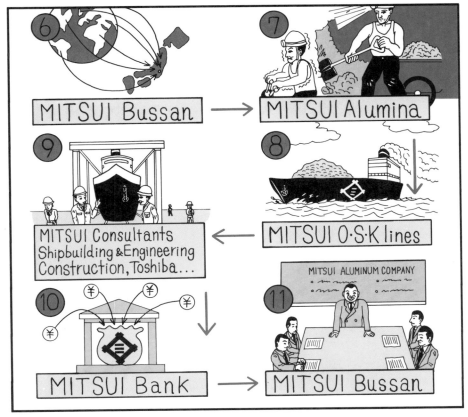

. . . in any part of the world. Taking a profit at every turn, it is always on the lookout for new ventures.

MORI BUILDING

One of Tokyo's
—and the world's—
largest private
real estate empires
is based on
a simple formula

Population density and rampant speculation have made Tokyo's land prices among the highest in the world. This adversely impacts the average citizen's quality of life in many ways. Commutes are longer as workers flee to cheaper suburbs. Villagelike areas and parkland in the inner city are replaced by concrete and tall sun-robbing structures. Fewer people can afford quality housing. Wealthy landowners grow more wealthy. Even the Hachikan Shrine in Ginza, for years sandwiched between office buildings, remodeled itself into an eight-story office tower to squeeze into its neighborhood.

Land in Tokyo is so precious that even a Shinto shrine is forced to go vertical and rent out office space.

A shopkeeper owned a *bento* (box lunch) shop in downtown Tokyo. He had been there for twenty-four years and was paying $1,200 rent a month. The land was now worth $13,000 per square foot. The building owner ordered the shopkeeper to move out, but the court upheld the tenancy. Then the owner moved thugs onto the third floor and parked a blaring sound truck in front to obstruct business. One Sunday morning in February 1988 the *bento* shop was smashed and ransacked—coincidentally, the day the lease was renewable—by ten men with sledgehammers. Such stories are not uncommon in Tokyo today.

Gangsters are used by greedy real estate companies to force tenants and owners out of prime development sites.

Taikichiro Mori, born in 1904, was the son of a rice merchant in downtown Tokyo. His father owned numerous rental properties in the neighborhood, and Taikichiro grew up learning the basics of real estate. Good-hearted and thoughtful, he became a Christian convert and studied philosophy. After seeing his father's holdings suddenly destroyed by earthquake and the resulting fire in 1923, he made "Don't think—act!" the motto of his life. He became a professor of economics and taught that the entrepreneur must contribute to society. After World War II, Mori received permission from his father to begin redeveloping the family property.

After the 1923 Tokyo earthquake, Taikichiro Mori tries to persuade his father to replace his rental houses with fireproof concrete structures.

Mori's first building went up in 1956. The next year up went Mori #2 and two years later Mori #3, each one larger than the one before. The postwar boom had begun, and there was a new need for modern office buildings. Mori had no trouble finding tenants and even used their deposits to finance construction. In the mid-1960s the market softened from overbuilding and a change in the tax laws. During this slow period, Mori reorganized his business. When conditions improved, he started building again—always blocklike concrete structures, always in the downtown area near Shinbashi and Toranomon in Minato Ward where he had grown up.

To secure a lease in a Mori building, Japan's national broadcasting company (NHK) sneaks in, in the middle of the night, with deposit money.

Mori has no gangster connections and believes that wealth follows naturally from good deeds. By focusing on only one section of Tokyo, he has been able to build up good connections and understanding among the people most affected by his business. Mori makes all his employees spend one year in a company dorm to learn about "human relationships," and his ten rules for success are read each morning before work. Mori has built most of his seventy-eight buildings without local resistance—and has seen his investments skyrocket in value.

Mori works with local people, who share in the profits of development, and teaches his employees to make human relations their number one concern.

In the 1960s the streets near the American Embassy in Tokyo were full of old wooden-frame houses and shops. Pressure was on for redevelopment. Mori bought some land for an office building nearby and, because of his local connections, soon found himself working with the city to build up the entire area at once rather than let it grow piecemeal. In 1969 Mori went to America to look at similar development models. Over the next dozen years he labored to win the support of 450 local landowners, most of whom eventually left the area.

The Golden Gateway Center in San Francisco is a model for Mori's greatest achievement—the giant mixed-use complex called Ark Hills.

Mori's dream complex was completed in 1986. Ark Hills consists of the Ark Mori Building, a thirty-seven-story "intelligent office building"; Ark Towers, with 500 apartments in three buildings; the ANA Hotel, with 900 rooms; the TV Asahi broadcast center; and Suntory Hall, with 2,006 seats. Mori screens his tenants carefully. The office tower has thirty tenants, seventeen of them foreign firms. Entertainers, gangster types, and night-shift workers are not allowed in the apartments. Mori believes that most of Tokyo will become like Ark Hills, with citizens living, working, and playing all on the same site.

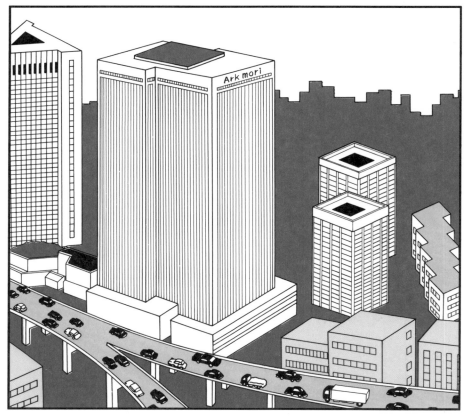

Ark Hills is built for $500 million and contains 3.5 million square feet of office, living, and public space.

Using floor space as a measure, Mori's is the third-largest construction company in Japan. Mori's total empire consists of four companies—building, development, tourism, and building management—worth, in 1987, some $15 billion. Mori himself is fabulously wealthy but leads a simple life. The key to his success is obvious: he cared about the neighborhood and lacked rapacity, even as he masterfully exploited the one fundamental aspect of land in Tokyo—its scarcity.

An indication of Mori's success (and Tokyo's land inflation) is Forbes magazine's listing of Mori as one of the richest men in the world.

TOKYO DISNEYLAND

The skeptics
said impossible,
but Japan's most popular
amusement complex
proves them wrong

The Oriental Land Company is a partnership between Mitsui Real Estate Development and the Keisei Electric Railway. Around 1960, the company asked Chiba Prefecture authorities to let it fill in part of Tokyo Bay in Urayasu City for new development. Chiba said yes, but only on condition that the new land be used for a major recreational facility. Mitsui preferred housing instead, but short of obtaining that, realized that a theme park would be better than, say, a baseball stadium. Masatomo Takahashi, whose father had been wartime governor of Taiwan, went to the local fishermen to obtain their consent. Landfill began in 1962.

Masatomo Takahashi persuades Urayasu fishermen to forfeit fishing rights so that a portion of Tokyo Bay can be land-filled.

In search of a model for their project, from 1966 to 1974 company representatives visited tourist, leisure, and recreational facilities around the world. They settled on Disneyland. In 1974 Oriental approached Walt Disney Productions. So did Mitsubishi, Mitsui's archrival, about a project on land near Mt. Fuji. Ron Cayo from Disney visited Japan in 1974 to look at both proposals. Over the course of the negotiations, mysteriously, Mitsubishi dropped out—perhaps as a result of government pressures ("your turn will come later"). Disney then did all the feasibility studies Mitsui needed at cost, confident that licensing would result in a big payoff.

For eight years, the Oriental Land Company scours the world looking for the right leisure facility prototype.

In Japanese fashion, Oriental Land would send fifteen negotiators to Disney's two. For the Japanese, a huge investment was at stake. Disney was optimistic about the profit potential, but the Mitsui people remained unenthusiastic. They had really wanted housing on the site, and their contract with Chiba said that if the leisure park didn't succeed the land could be sold off at a profit. Ron Cayo thought that Mitsui was just waiting for the deal to collapse. He presented Disney's basic thinking at the outset and many times came close to calling the talks off.

For three years, Oriental Land and Disney study and negotiate the deal. Many times, the talks almost break down.

Masatomo Takahashi, who had handled negotiations with the Urayasu fishermen, became vice-president of Oriental Land in 1975. Takahashi was a visionary who wanted a large-scale project that would leave his mark on history. He believed in the Disneyland concept, and he knew how much the Disney characters were loved in Japan. When talks broke down in 1977, Takahashi stepped in and, using all his political connections and adroit people skills, maneuvered to bring the two sides together. Today everyone takes credit for Tokyo Disneyland's success. But it was Takahashi who really saved the day.

Masatomo Takahashi, totally committed to the Disneyland project, manages the behind-the-scenes negotiations among the Japanese.

Construction began in December 1980. Over 100 Oriental Land managers went to the U.S. to learn how to run the park, while 200 Disney people worked on site in Japan. Tokyo Disneyland opened April 15, 1983. In return for its licensing and ongoing advice and expertise, Disney receives 10% of admissions and 5% of food and souvenir sales. Ron Cayo says getting the Japanese to understand Disney-style marketing has been difficult, but that the meticulous, image-conscious Japanese have been superb at operations and at preserving Disney's squeaky-clean image. Procedures are all laid out in volumes of Disney manuals, and strict adherence to these has been a big part of the project's success.

Disney provides its name, copyrights, ride and pavilion designs, engineering . . . and over 300 technical manuals.

Tokyo Disneyland has Adventureland, Fantasyland, Westernland, To-morrowland, Captain Eo, Big Thunder Mountain. . . but a few things are different. (1) A train ride direct from Disneyland to Tokyo Station takes twenty minutes. (2) It rains often in Japan, so Main Street has been covered in glass and renamed the World Bazaar. (3) Unique to Tokyo Disneyland is "Meet the World," an audioanimatronic show on the history of Japan. Originally the Japanese wanted only American food inside the park, but Japanese restaurants have been added for older guests. Almost all signs, however, are in English to preserve the all-American image. The park had 13 million visitors in 1988 and has generated over 100,000 jobs in Japan.

Tokyo Disneyland takes the best of America's Disneyland and Disney World and mixes in some special Japanese ingredients.

NISSIN FOODS

Late in life,
an entrepreneur
discovers the road
to success
is through
the Japanese stomach

Momofuku Ando was born of Japanese parents in Taiwan in 1911. When his parents died, Momofuku went to live with his grandparents, who were textile wholesalers. By the age of three Momofuku was learning the merchant's life, running errands and doing household chores. As a child, he spent his free time at the wholesale factory. When he was ten he left his grandparents to live alone with his younger sister. Momofuku did the laundry, butchered the chickens, and became an excellent cook, rising every day at dawn to make box lunches and get his sister ready for school.

By age eleven the self-reliant Momofuku Ando is living alone with his younger sister and taking care of her.

As a child, Ando wanted nothing more than to be a merchant. At age twenty-two he received his inheritance and immediately set himself up in Taiwan—a Japanese colony—as an importer of knitwear. He soon began a knitwear wholesaling operation in Osaka, where he established his headquarters and attended business school. Just before the war he entered the silkworm business, and then when the war began he sold arms and made fighter plane parts. Everything was an occasion for a new business. According to Ando, "an idea which cannot be commercialized is just a passing thought."

Ando soon becomes quite the young businessman, shuttling back and forth between his enterprises in Taiwan and Osaka.

During the war, Ando was framed by an employee and arrested by the military for black-marketing in materials used in making airplanes. Ando was tortured but maintained his innocence. Prison was grim. Six other men shared Ando's tiny, filthy cell. Ando, used to cleanliness, refused to eat. In his hunger, Ando realized that a human being is but an animal, no different from a pig. Ando began to eat again and after forty-five days was released. It had been a terrible ordeal, but Ando, always the business opportunist, had had a revelation about the importance of food.

While in military prison, a starved and weakened Ando realizes that, as regards food, a human is no different from a pig.

Out of jail, Ando began a slide projector factory, thinking slides could be used to educate the unskilled workers on which wartime industry increasingly relied. When the bombs began falling, Ando left Osaka and bought a mountain to supply charcoal, which he realized would be needed as fuel grew scarcer. At the end of the war, Ando found himself incredibly wealthy from insurance money collected on his bombed-out businesses in Osaka. Other Japanese were limited to only ¥50,000 compensation, but Ando had cleverly declared himself a Taiwanese national, on whom there were no such restrictions. He now had ¥40 million in cash.

Ando returns to business with his characteristic ferocity. One new enterprise is making charcoal—soon to be in great demand.

One year after the war ended, Ando went back to Osaka with his family. He began to buy land. The supply of land was always fixed, he reasoned, while industry's need for land would keep expanding. And land was cheap. One parcel Ando bought was near the ocean. Here he began to make salt, giving jobs to many indigent men. Next he bought three sardine fishing boats. Ando gave away salt and fish to the poor and out of work. He invited young people to his home and gave them money. He threw frequent birthday parties. Driving around in a big American Buick, Ando was like a king.

Now the richest man in Japan, Ando returns to Osaka to buy land and create new jobs with new businesses.

In 1948 Ando's company was capitalized at ¥5 million and was involved in seafood processing, textiles, salt, Western household goods, and publishing. In 1949 the company relocated to the center of Osaka—Japan's traditional merchant capital—and began a trading operation. In 1951 Ando, concerned about the plight of his undernourished countrymen, set up a laboratory to develop food supplements. The lab tried making protein tablets from frogs, cows, pigs, and chickens. The final product, called Bikuseiru, was approved by the government and sold to hospitals.

Ando establishes a nutrition and food lab for making protein tablets from frogs and chicken bones.

Ando, with his big car, entourage, and connections, raised suspicions. The Japanese police persuaded the American MPs to arrest him for tax evasion, saying that the money Ando gave away to local youth was actually disguised wages. The court sentenced Ando to four years hard labor, and the Osaka tax office seized his assets. In prison Ando hobnobbed with high-status war criminals and learned mahjongg. The food was American and tasty. In the meantime, Ando was countersuing the government, which finally agreed to his release after two years.

Ando, arrested for income tax evasion, ends up in jail again but this time finds it more to his liking: good food, interesting inmates, and mahjongg.

A free man, Ando next lent his name to a savings and loan association that was poorly managed and went bankrupt. In 1956 Ando was found guilty of breach of trust and was stripped of all he owned except his house. What to do next? He was over forty. In the alleys near the Hankyu Department Store in Osaka he saw the portable stalls that served bowls of wheat noodles, or *ramen*, doing a brisk business. America gave surplus wheat to Japan, so the Japanese government urged the citizenry to eat more bread. Ando thought ramen fit better with Japanese tastes. It was tasty, you didn't have to wait for it, and it was available everywhere. He would make ramen.

Middle-aged and bankrupt, Ando realizes that the popular ramen noodle stalls were onto a very good thing indeed.

Ando bought a noodle-making machine and began experimenting with a new "instant ramen." He discovered that prefrying would preserve the noodles and that the texture depended on the water content in the dough. But what flavoring should he use? One day his son accidentally got squirted with chicken blood. The son developed a strong aversion to chicken, but when Ando's mother-in-law put her noodles in chicken broth, he ate them right up. Ando figured if the flavor of chicken was that good, he should use it himself. Ando took samples of his packaged chicken-flavored instant ramen to a department store. They sold out in a day. It was 1958.

Working in his backyard shed, Ando tries to perfect his ramen noodles. In a fortuitous mishap, some chicken blood squirts his son in the face.

Ando moved his operations into an abandoned warehouse in Osaka and put his whole family to work. Ando, having been burned once, was leery of banks and credit and insisted on being paid in cash. Wholesalers resisted, but such was the demand that they had to accept. When Ando was making 20,000 packages a day, Mitsubishi approached him about becoming an exclusive wholesaler. Fearing takeover, Ando refused. In December 1958 he renamed his company Nissin Foods. The next spring he moved to a 60,000-square-foot plant. Mitsubishi still wanted in. Ando's deal: he would buy all his flour from them at ninety days and get paid cash-and-carry for his noodles.

Ando's chicken ramen is an "instant" success. Trucks literally circle the new factory waiting to haul the noodles to market.

In 1960 Ando opened his second factory. The following year saw three more factories, all of them paid for in cash. TV broadcasting had just begun, and Nissin's chicken ramen became one of the earliest sponsors of commercial programming in Japan. Sales by 1961 reached 550 million packages per year. Other companies, including big manufacturers like Meiji, began putting out competing products and luring away Nissin employees. Ando formed a ramen makers association to bring order to the market—and became its chairman. Sales soared to 2 billion units in 1963.

Ando, a tireless huckster, uses the new medium of TV and novel promotions like car parades with 100 brand-new Toyotas.

Looking for ways to improve and internationalize his product, Ando toured Europe and America in 1966. Ando knew that Westerners didn't eat with chopsticks, so he had to come up with a container that worked with a fork. In America, Ando learned about (1) bouillon base, (2) disposable paper cups, and (3) on the airplane home, sealed aluminum pouches with macadamia nuts. Taking a hint from these, Ando designed a coffee-cup-shaped container using styrofoam, which he imported and then manufactured in partnership with Dart Industries. He made the noodles thicker so they wouldn't break in the cup. And he added freeze-dried vegetables in foil packets.

In America, Ando gets three important hints for how to develop his new-style "Cup Noodle" instant ramen.

What a silly idea! Whoever heard of eating noodles with a fork from a styrofoam cup! In Japan, noodles came in a bowl and were eaten with chopsticks! And it was rude to eat while you walked! And ¥100 was far too expensive! So said the distributors. Ando countered by taking his new product to Tokyo's Ginza district on a busy shopping day. The students and teenagers loved it. So he put a hot-water vending machine on the Ginza. Then he installed Cup Noodle vending machines in schools and offices. The orders from distributors rolled in.

At first, Japanese food distributors think the new Cup Noodle concept is crazy, but Ando gets the young people hooked and business booms.

Ando's feasibility study showed that instant ramen wouldn't make it in America. Americans ate noodles like spaghetti, but not in a broth or with chopsticks. Ando didn't believe in the study. He believed in the product. So in 1968 he set up a U.S. factory anyway. He did modify the noodles, making them shorter (3 inches) so Americans wouldn't have to slurp. (Japanese love to noisily slurp noodles.) Called Top Ramen, Ando's noodles were a whole new product category for American consumers. In six years, Nissin Foods (U.S.A.) was in the black. Nissin now manufactures in ten countries.

In order to penetrate foreign markets, Ando considers differences in culture and eating habits—Americans don't like to slurp!

Nissin doesn't deal directly with stores. It sells its entire product line through three companies: Mitsubishi, C. Itoh, and Toshoku. Nissin's products in Hong Kong are sold by Mitsubishi's Hong Kong branch, sent on Mitsubishi shipping, insured by Mitsubishi insurance, trucked in Mitsubishi vehicles, and financed by loans from a Mitsubishi bank. Nissin buys its flour from Nisshin Flour Milling Company. Nisshin Flour pays Nissin to use its own name for the snack foods it produces, since Nissin registered the name in that category first. Nissin and Nisshin each own shares in the other.

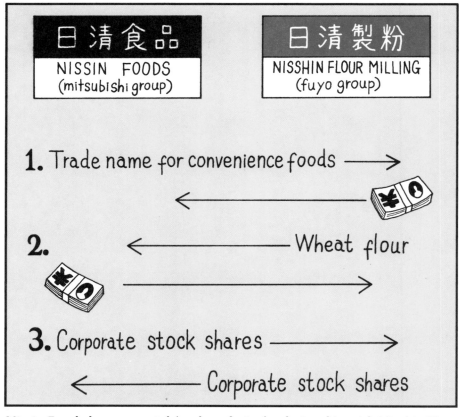

日清食品
NISSIN FOODS
(mitsubishi group)

日清製粉
NISSHIN FLOUR MILLING
(fuyo group)

1. Trade name for convenience foods ⟶
⟵

2. ⟵ Wheat flour
⟶

3. Corporate stock shares ⟶
⟵ Corporate stock shares

Nissin Foods has a special (and confusing) relationship with Nisshin Flour Milling Company, a distinguished older firm.

In 1974 Nissin introduced instant rice in a cup. This was a huge failure. With rice readily available at home, no one needed it. But the company made it all back in 1976 with its instant chow mein. In 1981 Ando, age seventy-one, became chairman. His first son took over as president, but in two years his father fired him (for preferring natural foods). In 1985 Ando's second son became president at age thirty-seven. In 1988 the company opened its new Tokyo headquarters, called the Foodeum, at a cost of $160 million. Located in Shinjuku, a shopping and recreation area, the building is designed to generate interest in noodles and bring the company closer to its customers.

An enduring monument to the noodle, Nissin's new headquarters boasts Italian and ramen restaurants, a ramen museum, and a two-story disco.

FOX BAGELS

An American expatriate
transplants an
exotic ethnic edible
into the Tokyo
food scene

Lyle Fox, an American raised in Chicago, completed his studies at the FALCON (Full Year Asian Language Concentration) program at Cornell University in 1979. FALCON had been a grueling experience—six hours a day for twelve months—but now it was over, and Lyle, his teacher, and five others in his class got money from the Japan Foundation to go to Japan to continue their studies for the summer. After the summer, three students went home and three stayed in Japan, among them Lyle. No job was waiting for him back in America, and it was time to put all that hard-won education to use.

In 1979 Lyle Fox visits Japan with fellow students from his Cornell University Japanese-language class.

Business opportunities for Americans living in Japan were limited to teaching, editing, copywriting, and other jobs related to the ability to speak and write English. Lyle taught English a bit and took a job as a proofreader at the English-language *Japan Times*. When a competitor newspaper, the *Daily Yomiuri*, offered him more pay, he went there. But Lyle quickly became disillusioned with the timid Japanese press and the way information was controlled in Japan. To Lyle, the English-language papers were just for show and had no clout at all.

In Japan, Lyle supports himself as an English teacher and as a proof-reader/copywriter for an English-language newspaper.

Near Lyle's apartment was a *yakitori* (grilled chicken) shop run by a Russian who was a Japanese citizen. Lyle would hang out there and talk to the owner about food. Lyle had worked in restaurants in America and liked to cook. He and the Russian decided to open a new place that would offer a mixture of Italian, Russian, and Jewish cuisine—and a take-out bagel counter. Lyle quit his job. Then his partner pulled out. But Lyle couldn't get the dream of bagels out of his head. And he didn't want to go back to the newspaper. He would push on alone—except he knew nothing at all about business.

Lyle becomes friendly with the owner of a local grilled chicken shop, and together they plan a new international cuisine restaurant.

Lyle's wife, a Japanese woman he had met at the *yakitori* shop, had a friend who was an accountant. He sat down with Lyle to discuss finances and a business plan. Lyle didn't know but figured, well, the American Club, foreign airline staff, embassies, they'll all buy bagels, and came up with an estimated sales figure. He borrowed ¥2 million ($10,000 at the time) and rented a 150-square-foot space for his factory. He bought all his equipment on credit—not knowing how to make bagels, though, he ended up buying the wrong kind of mixer. Lyle's wife tended the books.

Lyle pursues his dream, but when it comes time to buy equipment he realizes he doesn't have the foggiest idea of even how to make a bagel.

Lyle's Russian ex-partner had seen a CBS News piece about a man in North Carolina who made bagels with rice flour. Thinking this would be perfect for Japan, Lyle wrote to him. The man wrote back with his complete recipe and instructions. Lyle practiced and wrote again whenever he had problems. The man replied thoughtfully and in detail. In three months, Lyle had mastered the bagel. For ingredients, Lyle went to a local shopkeeper, who was more than happy to introduce him to wholesalers. The suppliers were equally eager to help Lyle get his business started.

Lyle corresponds with a kindly man in North Carolina, who in his letters gives him a complete course in bagel making.

Calling his company Fox Bagels, Lyle approached the stores that cater to foreigners. One of them, National Azabu, agreed to try his bagels, and ended up buying two hundred a day. After the New York Festival at Seibu Department Store in Shibuya, Lyle was invited to sell his bagels at the store on a regular basis, and this got him into other big department stores in Tokyo. A Japanese importer of dry-cleaning equipment from Sweden, thanks to its one American employee who was crazy about bagels, agreed to loan Lyle money and guarantee the lease on a new shop and equipment.

As a promotion, Lyle presents his bagels at the prestigious Seibu Department Store's New York Festival. They are a big hit.

Lyle's workspace was so small he couldn't make and bake at the same time, so he worked around the clock. His orders were increasing. Lyle's brother and his wife came from America to help, but left after a year. The foreign students Lyle hired made mistakes. Lyle gave up. He farmed out the baking to a medium-sized bakery. Lyle phoned in the orders every day and got the bagels at 4 a.m. But the bagels were hard to make, and the baker wanted to quit. So he introduced Lyle to another baker, who bought all the equipment and is still baking with Lyle to this day.

After a few years of backbreaking work, Lyle subcontracts out the bagel making to a Japanese bakery so that he can concentrate on marketing.

(1) Lyle's bagels are about 10% smaller than American bagels. (2) They're also softer (Japanese like soft bready textures). (3) About 70% of what Japanese buy in bakeries is sweets, not bread. Since his cinnamon raisin outsells his plain, sesame, and onion bagels among the Japanese, Lyle is thinking of adding new dessertlike "flavors." (4) One obstacle to greater growth is the Japanese unfamiliarity with bagels. In his shop, Lyle keeps the toaster on all day so he can give instant demonstrations with delicious cream cheese spreads.

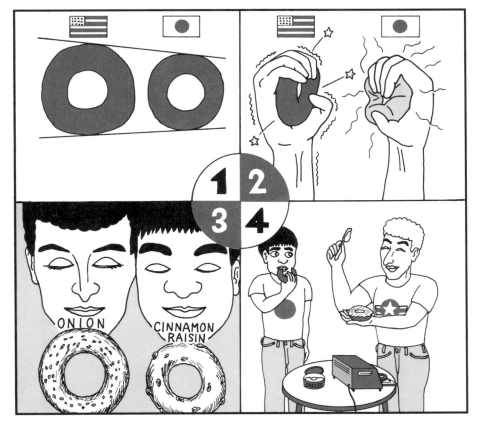

Because Japanese people have no fixed notion of what a bagel is, Lyle has to educate the consumer and adapt his product to Japanese tastes.

Pasco, one of Japan's largest baked-goods manufacturers, decided to enter the bagel business and sent spies to Lyle's shop. They imported a bagel machine like Lyle's and, through a mutual contact, asked Lyle to help set up the machine. Lyle at first worried about the competition but then realized two things. First, Pasco would spend time and money developing the bagel market in Japan, something Lyle couldn't afford to do by himself, and second, Pasco's bagels would never be as good as his own. Lyle spent two days working in the Pasco factory.

To increase public awareness and develop the bagel market in Japan, Lyle helps his arch-rival get its bagel-forming machine working.

Lyle makes over 5,000 bagels a day and has thirty employees. (1) He has begun selling frozen bagel dough to other bakers who can bake and repackage it at their convenience. (2) For variety, he has added bagel dogs, cheesecake, brownies, and dill pickles. (3) His newest venture is Wall Street Sandwiches, an American-style delicatessen delivery service. The company first targeted foreign securities traders in the Ark Hills area of Tokyo but has gradually expanded throughout the business districts. Now 40% of the customers are Japanese. Orders are accepted by fax.

Lyle now sells frozen bagels, bagel novelty items (bagel dogs and bagel chips), and deli-style sandwiches delivered to your office.

SHISEIDO

Japan's largest
cosmetics company
remains true to
its Japanese-
European
aesthetic legacy

Yushin Fukuhara's father was skilled in Chinese herbal medicine. It was 1865, and Japan was just beginning to study Western culture and science. Yushin, then eighteen, went off to Tokyo to become one of the first Japanese to study Western pharmacology. After graduation he entered the Naval Hospital, where he became director of the Pharmaceutical Bureau. Unable to tolerate the narrow bureaucratic mentality and militaristic attitudes of the navy, Yushin grew dissatisfied with his work and, at age twenty-five, quit to open his own pharmacy.

Yushin Fukuhara is not happy working as director of the Pharmaceutical Bureau of the Japanese Imperial Navy.

Yushin's shop was called Fukuhara Shiseido. Located in Tokyo's chic Ginza district, it was the first Western-style pharmacy in Japan. The company was cross-cultural from the beginning, employing Western management techniques and products but guided by Chinese Confucian philosophy. The name Shiseido is based on Chinese characters from a popular text at the time that contains the phrase: "How surpassing is the virtue of the Earth from which all things are born. This virtue of the Earth combines with the virtue of Heaven to make all things grow."

Yushin begins Japan's first Western-style pharmacy in 1872 in Tokyo's Ginza district.

Most of Yushin's customers were either nobility or rich people who were attuned to the new clothes and ideas entering Japan from the West. Shiseido began selling cosmetics as well as medicines. In 1888 it introduced Japan's first toothpaste, and in 1897 it brought out Eudermine, an astringent skin lotion still sold today. Yushin went abroad in 1900. In Paris he became further enamored of Western culture, and in New York he discovered the drugstore and soda fountain. In 1902 Yushin brought this new concept back to his Ginza shop (it took two months to deliver the soda glasses by boat), and it was an instant hit.

Yushin's fashionable pharmacy even has an American-style soda fountain.

Yushin's first son was sickly, and his second son died. His third son, Shinzo, wanted to be an artist but Yushin insisted he learn the family trade. Shinzo was sent to New York to study pharmacology at Columbia University. After graduation he apprenticed at a drugstore at Broadway and 33rd, and then worked as a chemist for two years at a cosmetics factory in Yonkers. While in New York he met Noboru Matsumoto, who was working at Simpson-Crawford Department Store while studying marketing at NYU. Matsumoto would later join Shiseido, offering cool and rational business leadership that perfectly complemented Shinzo's artistic vision.

In New York, Yushin's son Shinzo studies pharmacology and meets another Japanese studying American management techniques.

In 1913 Shinzo left New York for Europe to study the cosmetics and fashion industries. He visited art museums and took impressionistic photographs, and he befriended (and helped support) many expatriate Japanese artists, some of whom later joined Shiseido's design staff. Shinzo had enormous artistic sensitivity, and when he returned to Japan he took over the pharmacy and began to emphasize cosmetics, in his words a "dream" product, over mere medicines. He created the first Western-style line of makeup and lotion, combining his knowledge of chemistry with his ideals of beauty. He made face powder in seven shades instead of what then existed, only white.

Shinzo goes to Europe and indulges his artistic impulses, becoming one of Japan's first fine art photographers.

In 1915, at age thirty-two, Shinzo became president of Shiseido. In 1917, Noboru Matsumoto was hired as sales director and de facto operations chief so that Shinzo could focus on design and marketing. Early on, Shinzo understood the importance of corporate image and packaging. He designed the company's camellia trademark. He made sure the words "Shiseido, Ginza, Tokyo" appeared on every package to give the company status. He employed his favored arabesque, rococo, and art nouveau designs to suggest the richness and modernity of the European image to Japanese consumers. All this was quite revolutionary in Japan at the time.

Shinzo designs the enduring camellia trademark as his artistic nature sets the tone for Shiseido's packaging and marketing.

With an abiding interest in New York and Paris style, Shinzo continued to bring Western design, custom, and culture to Japan. To better educate the Japanese public in such matters, Shinzo began a monthly magazine, *Hanatsubaki*. He also brought the first hair dryer to Japan. He brought in a beautician from America, whose "telephone" style (called *mimika-kushi*, or "ear hiding") created a rage. A huge earthquake in Tokyo in 1923 frightened the beautician away, however. The same earthquake also destroyed the summer villa Frank Lloyd Wright had designed for Shinzo in the nearby mountains of Hakone.

The 1923 Tokyo earthquake destroys Shinzo's villa and scares the daylights out of the hair stylist he had imported from America.

Shiseido could not make cosmetics during the war, only medicine and other essentials. After the war, the company was almost bankrupt. In 1946 it returned to cosmetics production with cheap nail enamel. The same year it produced the first printed color poster after the war, showing Setsuko Hana, an actress with a pure, virgin image that summed up Japan's hopes for the future. In 1948 Shinzo died, and his brother's son became president. In 1951, before European and American high-end products entered Japan, Shiseido began a new line of luxury products called "de Luxe." By 1956 Shiseido was the number one cosmetics company in Japan.

Immediately after the war, Shiseido uses posters to establish the company's image. Its first postwar product is nail polish.

Shiseido is pushing strongly into foreign markets, which now account for more than 10% of annual revenues. Taiwan Shiseido was formed in 1955, followed by outlets in Honolulu, Italy, and, in 1965, the continental U.S. In 1979 Shiseido hired Serge Lutens, previously with Christian Dior, to help craft the company's international image. Lutens based his campaign on the Silk Road and Roland Barthes's *Empire of Signs*, and instead of using a color or floral motif, as was customary in cosmetics ads, he used a circle as the unifying theme. The model Sayoko Yamaguchi became famous as a result of these ads.

Foreign markets are increasingly important. A French photographer and makeup artist is hired to develop Shiseido's international image.

Japan's population is rapidly aging. President Yoshiharu Fukuhara sees Shiseido becoming less reliant on cosmetics (now 80% of sales) and promoting instead the idea of growing old "cleverly, beautifully, gracefully." The company today operates beauty parlors, clothing boutiques, restaurants, a "beauty research institute," and fitness clubs, and it has set up a biotech lab to develop over-the-counter drugs for the elderly. Shiseido maintains the largest in-house ad department in Japan (130 people) and, with sales of $2.8 billion and 25,000 employees, is the third-largest cosmetics company in the world.

Yoshiharu Fukuhara, president since 1987, heads a diversified enterprise designed for an increasingly older and sophisticated population.

FOLIO

A cleverly managed
model agency
based on the
Japanese yen
for Western beauty

Upon college graduation, Hiroshi Aoyagi began working at the McCann Erickson–Hakuhodo advertising agency in Tokyo. For eight years he handled the Nescafé instant coffee account. Aoyagi worked hard, but when he realized he was not first in line for promotion, he quit. In 1968, with $5,000 in savings and an American friend, he started an import business. The idea was to bring in California cantaloupes that cost only $1 but looked like the $80 gift-wrapped Japanese musk melons sold in department stores. But half the fruit rotted in transport, and Aoyagi lost money.

After working for the same Tokyo ad agency for eight years, Hiroshi Aoyagi realizes his prospects for corporate advancement are limited.

Aoyagi decided to focus on the service sector, where a small business had a chance of succeeding. Aoyagi had many foreign model friends, and they often complained to him about their problems working in Japan—not being paid, being expected to "act Japanese," the language barrier. At a party in 1977, Aoyagi met Paul Rose, a British ex–foreign model who was living in Japan with his Danish wife (a model who was having problems with her agency). Aoyagi told Paul he'd put up the money for a new agency, and Paul could run it for a 30% share. The Folio model agency was born in 1978.

From his foreign model friends, Aoyagi hears about the problems of foreign models in Japan and gets an idea for a new business.

Around this time Aoyagi traveled to New York to explore the famous Ford Modeling Agency. He was impressed by Ford's image, high profile, and reputation for quality and honesty. This was in marked contrast to Japan, where running a modeling agency was a sleazy profession associated with gangsters and creative bookkeeping. Aoyagi returned to Tokyo determined to achieve for Folio the same kind of prestige that Ford had around the world. Today Folio has the classiest image of all agencies in Japan. It prides itself on being up-front and aboveboard in all business dealings with its models.

On a visit to New York, Aoyagi is astonished that a modeling agency can be respectable, prestigious, and profitable all at the same time.

To be efficient, punctual, and trustworthy with money—these were Aoyagi's goals. The first American models he brought in were from Los Angeles agencies. The girls—some as young as fifteen—came to Tokyo feeling very insecure. Folio helped the girls with their living arrangements, attended to their emotional needs, and reassured their parents. All the Folio staff were bilingual, including the sales force. Other agencies had "bookers," who merely took orders over the phone. Folio salespeople, however, actually made the rounds of prospective clients' offices to introduce the new models in town.

Folio is run like an international company with Western-style management. All its employees speak English and Japanese.

The average age of a Folio foreign model is nineteen. Each girl (there are some male models too) who comes to Japan is guaranteed $4,000 a month minimum; the average makes $15,000 and some make as much as $50,000. The money and the good experience make Folio *the* place to work in Tokyo, and the company ranks among the top five agencies in the world in billings. Folio has now begun exporting Japanese models to Paris and New York. Aoyagi says that Japanese economic power has created a new demand for the Asian look in the West.

Folio has achieved respectability and profitability in Japan and is also very rewarding for the foreign models it handles.

The Folio businesses gross about $100 million a year, but Aoyagi draws a salary of only $500,000, preferring to reinvest most of his profit in new ventures. He has begun the Folio Tennis Club (with tournament surfaces), a typesetting firm, an ad agency, and a PR firm that brought the musical *42nd Street* to Japan. His company Studio Folio owns photography studios. The studio in Tokyo's Roppongi district has wooden floors, artificial and daylight studios, and a makeup room, and was specially designed for fashion shoots. Aoyagi spends several months a year relaxing in Hawaii, where he dabbles in real estate to stay productive even on vacation.

Hiroshi Aoyagi's business universe now includes an ad agency, rental studios, a tennis club, a PR firm, and Hawaiian real estate.

DENTSU

The world's largest
advertising agency
and Japan's
media broker and
mega-event planner

A journalist during the Sino-Japanese War in the 1890s, Hoshiro Mitsunaga was upset that his stories from the front lines took so long to get through. Foreign wire services, he discovered, monopolized the news and presented Japanese readers with Western biases. Japanese newspapers, short of cash and beholden to politicians, could do little to change the situation. Mitsunaga reasoned that if he could generate advertising revenue for the papers they would be able to afford a new, Japanese wire service. So at age thirty-six he set up two separate companies, one to handle advertising, the other to provide the news.

In 1901 a young man begins two companies in Tokyo—an ad agency and a news wire service.

Mitsunaga's first clients were small local newspapers that were always slow in paying. Instead of billing separately for the ads and the news service, Mitsunaga decided to combine the two, thus allowing the papers to pay for the news not with cash but with ad space, which Mitsunaga could then profitably sell to businesses. In 1907 Mitsunaga created Nippon Denpo Tsushin-sha—or Dentsu for short—from his two existing companies. The next year he contracted to provide Japan with the UP (now UPI) wire service. Papers that signed on came to depend on Dentsu for news coverage, and Dentsu in turn squeezed them for favorable ad rates, which it used to attract clients.

Mitsunaga uses the merger of his companies to trade delinquent payments to his news agency for advertising space.

In 1936, in order to control public information, Japan's military leaders declared that henceforth Dentsu and all other news services would be combined into a single quasi-governmental agency, called Domei. To add insult to injury, the government also directed Dentsu to turn 50% of all its stock over to Domei, for which Dentsu got nothing in return. Then in 1943 the government forced the nation's 186 ad agencies to reduce their number to 12. Working behind the scenes on this deal, however, was Hideo Yoshida, Dentsu's managing director—and of the final 12 agencies, 4 ended up under Dentsu's direct control.

Japan's military rulers order Mitsunaga, now age seventy, to give up the news agency along with half of all Dentsu stock.

Having lost its news agency, Dentsu had to work extra hard to survive, particularly when Japan's defeat was imminent and there was a shortage of money, consumer goods, newsprint, and optimism. Mitsunaga, a truly inspirational leader, rallied his troops to fight on anyway. His salesmen paid regular visits to their clients, picking their way through rubble-filled streets, even when they knew there was no business to be found. Mitsunaga realized that, in Japan, connections were everything, and that when the war was over his patient troops would have the advantage.

Tokyo is ravaged by fire bombs, but Dentsu employees remain loyal to their founder's motto and keep stroking their clients and looking for business.

As a quasi-governmental information agency, Domei was viewed with suspicion by the Americans, who favored a free press in Japan. Domei dissolved itself, and its officers reformed into a new news agency, called Kyodo, in October 1945. Dentsu, gearing up to rebuild its own news agency around UP, demanded that the Dentsu stock Domei had forcibly seized now be returned. But the ex-president of Domei arranged for the Dentsu stock to go to Kyodo instead, in a highly questionable transaction. Jiji Press, also formed by ex-Domei officers, got 18% of the Dentsu stock, and another 4% stayed in the hands of the Domei caretaker.

The disposition of Dentsu stock after the war is a bit shady, but it gets by the Occupation authorities.

Their ownership of so much Dentsu stock gave Kyodo and Jiji Press an inordinate amount of control over Dentsu's activities. A solution was arranged by which Dentsu agreed never again to attempt to start up a news agency and Kyodo and Jiji agreed to stay out of the advertising business. This agreement was never written down, but it has been honored by all sides to this day. A separate committee oversees ownership of Dentsu's own stock, which is scattered among various small shareholders. Today Kyodo owns 28.3% of Dentsu, and Jiji owns 20.1%.

A solution to the Dentsu stock ownership problem is worked out among the principals in typically harmonious Japanese style.

Hideo Yoshida became Dentsu's fourth president in 1947. He was known in Japan as the "demon of advertising" for his drive, tenacity, and daring. He helped establish the first commercial radio and TV stations in Japan (not incidentally a great place to sell ads), and he helped engineer public support for the Japanese government that took over from the Occupation. Yoshida hired many "unhirable" executives whom the Americans had removed from their posts at large companies. These men not only retained connections with their former colleagues, but they had superb management skills that would help Dentsu grow and prosper.

Dentsu's new CEO hires purged executives as "consultants" to give him an inside track to the upper ranks of their former companies.

Publishing and broadcast media depend on advertising for their survival. In the opinion of some critics, Dentsu's high-level connections and its 23% share of the ad market in Japan have given it undue influence over the content of these media. A recent exposé tells (without naming names) how Dentsu will approach a target company with the threat to publicize a personal or financial scandal in the newsweeklies. The company will then "suddenly" announce that its ad account has moved to Dentsu—and nothing of the scandal will ever appear in public.

Dentsu is respected but feared. Critics say it starts "fires" (scandals) and then offers to put them out in return for a company's ad account.

Dentsu's forte is the multimedia event. Its first such venture was the Osaka Expo of 1970, which promoted business interests and led to the construction of new roads, parkland, and commercial development. In 1985 Dentsu worked with the government at the Tsukuba Science Expo to promote high-tech awareness to the Japanese people. In 1984 and 1988, Dentsu handled all the Olympic sponsorship and licensing deals in Japan. Dentsu also produces movies and uses its stars and characters to offer its clients advertising tie-ins, merchandise sales, and other promotional opportunities.

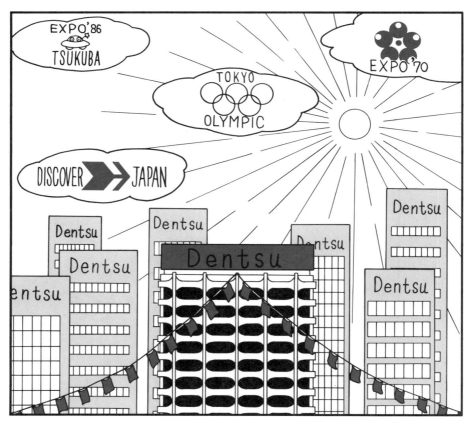

Dentsu's power and connections enable it to take on promotional projects of enormous size and financial and cultural impact.

Dentsu has thirty-one account and six creative divisions scattered throughout eleven separate buildings in the area surrounding its Tokyo corporate headquarters. This compartmentalization allows Dentsu to take on the accounts of competing clients. Dentsu handles a total of 3,300 accounts, including all the major beer, automobile, and cosmetic companies in Japan. It says competing clients benefit from (1) the cost-effectiveness of not having to do basic research twice and (2) Dentsu's huge media clout. And it guarantees that there is no collusion between account reps. But this practice poses problems as Dentsu develops the overseas business it needs for future growth.

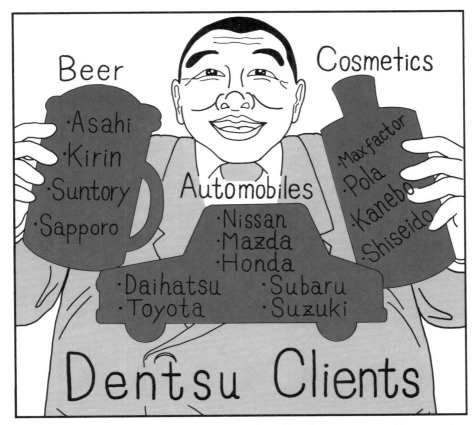

Unlike ad agencies elsewhere, Dentsu handles the accounts of competing clients. The clients don't like it, but what can they do?

MUJIRUSHI RYOHIN

The American
generic goods concept
is skillfully restyled
and marketed into
a fashionable business

The Japanese have always been sensitive to what Western marketers call "added value." Packaging, brand name, design, and advertising are as important as the intrinsic value of the product. In the consumerist frenzy of the 1970s, Japanese bought expensive brand name items because they were supposed to be "the best." By the end of the decade, Japanese consumers—now able to afford anything—retrenched. They wanted quality, substance, economy. They even began to eat natural foods. Genuineness and plainness would become the new "added values."

In the late 1970s, Japanese consumers become obsessed with high style, heavy design statements, and brand name goods.

Seiyu, a low-priced chain of department and food stores owned by the Seibu Department Store group, hired a design team to create a new house brand for their stores. On a trip to America, one of the team was looking for beer cans for a collector friend in Japan. In a grocery she discovered generic beer and other goods. She liked the simple, unaffected design of the packaging. Back in Japan, the Seiyu team took the concept and restyled and refined it to express the essence of "generic." Without a brand name, the product could appeal to the consumer's sense of individuality.

A member of Seiyu's concept development team discovers generic packaging while shopping at an American supermarket.

The name Mujirushi Ryohin means "No Brand, Good Product." The concept is tinged with idealistic romanticism. The cheapness, plain function, and open and honest packaging of MR products represent Japan's postwar social virtues. To find useful goods that challenged consumer sensibilities, MR buyers scoured the world. Cotton from Peru, previously used only for sweat socks, was used for casual knitwear. Food parts normally thrown away, like salmon heads, were offered for their nutrition and value. MR's first forty products came out in 1980. Among the big hits were freeze-dried coffee and broken shiitake mushroom pieces.

Mujirushi Ryohin offers discerning consumers high-quality, low-cost, "generic chic" items from all over the world.

MR packaging suggests that the energy and resources of the company have gone into the product and nowhere else. A label (of brown recycled paper) tells why the product is cheap, to allay fears that there is something wrong with it. The MR name, written in Sino-Japanese characters, bucks the trend of using Western-sounding names in retailing. It suggests Japaneseness and the high-quality goods of daily life in a time gone by. Eliminating the excessive packaging gives consumers credit for having intelligence. And, in a changing but still traditional Japan, no-brandness is a means of polite, thoughtful rebellion.

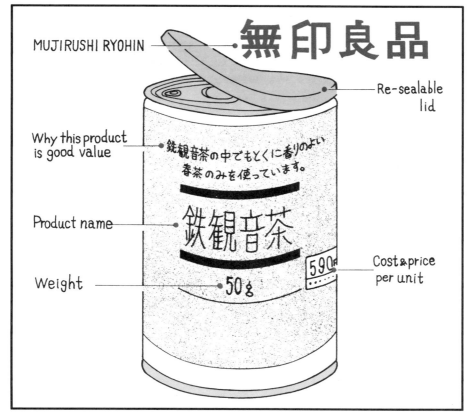

The company presents its products with honest labels on plain packages that are a study in stylish antistyle.

Seiyu's consumer base was located in the suburbs, but the MR concept team suggested that a store devoted exclusively to MR products be built in trendy Aoyama in central Tokyo. Aoyama was chosen (1) to give the MR line some of Aoyama's stylish "added value" without having to compromise the plainness of the product itself and (2) to attract the attention of the many editors and journalists who frequented the area. The new store reflected the MR image: recycled wood floors, recycled tiles, plain shelves that let consumers touch and see everything. The store realized its first year's sales goal in its first month.

In 1983 MR opens its first freestanding store in the ultrafashionable, style-setting Tokyo district of Aoyama.

MR used posters to promote its image. Its first poster campaign, in 1981, read "Good personality products you can proudly tell others you bought at Mujirushi Ryohin" and showed unprocessed paper cups, recycled memo pads, hotel-quality towels, mushroom fragments, a bicycle with replaceable parts. By 1985 MR had become a phenomenon. Sales hit $250 million and climbed to $285 million in 1988. The problem, of course, is that as sales go up, production increases. After a while, MR has bought up all the mushroom fragments to be had and must buy whole mushrooms to break into new fragments. What's cheap and unprocessed about that?

The MR ideology is communicated through posters with phrases like "Love is Unadorned" and the slightly ironic "Individual Mujirushi Ryohin."

URASENKE

A generations-old
tea ceremony school is
also a money-making
modern business

When young priest Murata Shuko (1422–1502) was expelled from his temple for laziness, he went to a doctor, who advised him to drink plenty of tea as a stimulant. Monks in China and Japan had been drinking tea for centuries to help them stay awake during meditation. Shuko began regularly offering tea to his visitors. The shogun Ashikaga Yoshimasa liked this idea and built for Shuko a tea hut. It was here that Shuko added to tea drinking the idea of cooking a meal and serving it with formality, conversation, and verse composition. All the cultured folk flocked to seek the favor of Shuko, Japan's first tea master.

Murata Shuko keeps falling asleep at the temple and is given a prescription of tea to help him stay awake.

Sen no Rikyu, born in 1522, was the son of a fish wholesaler. At seventeen he developed an interest in tea. His eloquence and aptitude eventually attracted the attention of Nobunaga, the most powerful warrior in Japan at the time. Under Nobunaga's patronage, Rikyu became the leading tea master in Japan. It was he who codified and developed tea drinking into a ritual ceremony. He infused tea culture with the aesthetic of simple, elegant poverty and drew from all of Japan's artistic traditions—poetry, flower arranging, architecture, ceramics. Under Rikyu, the teahouse became a place where the cares of the world could be left behind.

Sen no Rikyu becomes adviser to the great warlord Nobunaga on the utensils, practice, and aesthetic of tea.

Nobunaga was assassinated in 1582. Rikyu entered the service of his successor, Hideyoshi. Hideyoshi was a great fan of tea, and under his patronage tea attracted a wide following among court aristocrats, warriors, feudal lords, and wealthy commoners. Tea ceremonies were held at war encampments for refreshment and amusement. Even Christian churches had tearooms (it is said that paraphernalia for the Catholic Mass influenced tea rituals and utensils). Rikyu developed rules for placement of objects, treatment of guests, and gestures, and his innovations continue to influence Japanese art and social behavior today.

Rikyu loves "performance." He puts Japanese pillows on stones before a snow and the next day removes them to reveal a path to the teahouse.

In the otherworldly atmosphere of the tearoom, the tea ceremony became a tiny stage on which many political dramas were delicately enacted. At one gathering, Hideyoshi brought out some of the dead Nobunaga's utensils, implying that it was he who was now in charge. Hideyoshi sought political alliances in the tearoom and used tea parties to celebrate his battlefield triumphs. He restricted the right to conduct tea parties and made participation in tea a symbol of submission to his rule. All warriors learned the art of tea. At the center was Rikyu, a cultural arbiter and, more importantly, a diplomatic middleman when Hideyoshi needed one.

Tea offers Japan's leaders "drinks with the boys" and the chance to discuss strategies in nonthreatening surroundings.

Hideyoshi and the tea master Rikyu had a falling out. Some say it was because Rikyu refused to allow his widowed daughter (a Catholic) to become Hideyoshi's concubine, or because Rikyu controlled the market for new tea utensils and sold them at unconscionably high prices, or because he was disrespectful and increasingly independent. Whatever the reason, in 1591 Hideyoshi exiled Rikyu from the capital, and then a week later brought him back surrounded by 3,000 soldiers and ordered him to slit his own belly and die. Rikyu's second stood by to cut off his head. Hideyoshi is said to have later regretted his decision.

Hideyoshi forces Rikyu to commit ritual suicide—and to this day no one is sure exactly why.

The repentant Hideyoshi returned property, some money, and permission to use the family name to Sotan, Rikyu's grandson. Sotan refused to become involved in politics and instead concentrated on performing so-called *wabi* tea, which reflected the ideals of simplicity and rustic poverty (in contrast to *daimyo* tea, practiced by warriors, which was more ornate and elaborate). One of Sotan's four sons turned his back on the family tradition, but the other three all formed their own tea schools upon their father's retirement. The most successful of these schools would be the one founded by Soshitsu and called Urasenke.

Rikyu's grandson, Sotan, has four sons, three of whom go on to found tea schools that still exist today.

In Japan, masters of traditional arts like flower arranging, calligraphy—and tea—are not self-taught. They study with teachers who belong to one or another school, or style, of practice. The head of the school is called the *iemoto*. New students gradually work their way up the school hierarchy, paying money at each stage—and thus generating enormous profits at the top of the pyramid. The *iemoto* system for tea was established in the 18th century by a seventh-generation descendant of Rikyu who liked to perform the tea ceremony naked on hot summer days.

*The **iemoto** system in Japan organizes art into a pyramid scheme by which higher ranks profit from "sales" made by lower recruits.*

The tea schools, based in Kyoto, fell upon hard times after the Meiji Restoration of 1868 and the move of the imperial capital to Tokyo. To survive in a modernizing Japan the tea masters added theatrical and Western elements, among them chairs and a quicker, more tolerable "mini-ceremony." Around 1900 Ennosai Tetchu of Urasenke developed the idea of marketing tea as charm-school training to classes of students at a girls' school in Kyoto. Prior to this time most students of tea had been males, but Ennosai's idea caught on, and today most practitioners of tea are women.

In the early 1900s, studying Urasenke-style tea becomes part of the requisite education for prospective Japanese brides.

Kayoko, daughter of a poor maid, married Tantansai, successor to the Urasenke grand mastership, in 1921. The modest Tantansai confined himself to tea, while Kayoko was a genius promoter for the tea business. (1) She tipped lavishly and spread money around. (2) She got the mayor of Kyoto to switch from sake to tea, and became a force in local politics. (3) She invited U.S. Occupation officers to highly publicized tea ceremonies. She also convinced big hotels to put in Urasenke-style tearooms, and she married her children into families of powerful politicians, financiers, and artists.

Kayoko, wife of the fourteenth iemoto, establishes Urasenke as the leading school of tea by adroit use of money, connections, and favors.

Soshitsu was raised by his mother and had the reputation of being a bit of a brat. A pilot during the war, he was all set to fly on a suicide mission when he received orders not to go. Everyone else perished. When Soshitsu returned home after the war he found his father serving tea to an American. "The war is over," his father said, adding that the only way to avoid conflict is for people to get to know each other. Since then, Soshitsu has devoted himself to world peace. At age twenty-seven he became the first Urasenke tea person to go abroad. In 1965 he became the fifteenth *iemoto*.

Kayoko's son, Soshitsu, trains as a kamikaze pilot and makes tea for his buddies before they take off.

In 1961, after Soshitsu returned from his second trip to the U.S., he joined the Kyoto Junior Chamber of Commerce. Later he became vice-chairman of the national group. Here he got acquainted with the Robunkai, a group of businessmen seriously devoted to the practice of tea. Soshitsu managed to bring top politicians and businessmen into the group and to elevate Robunkai's status within the Urasenke organization. Robunkai members contribute and consult to Urasenke, and have helped build the school into a complex business conglomerate.

Blessed with the same promotional acumen as his mother, Soshitsu enlists the captains of industry to his side through the practice of tea.

Because of the marriages his mother engineered, Soshitsu has relatives well placed in industry, politics, academia, and the mass media. His own son married into the imperial family. A connection with Soshitsu and his school is a sought-after prize. In 1985 the first New Year's teas at Urasenke were held over seven days and drew 2,000 people to Kyoto. In 1986 Soshitsu gave a tea for the wives of visiting Tokyo Summit leaders. Honored by foreign nations, and highly visible in his own country, Soshitsu occupies a unique position in the Japanese power loop.

Soshitsu becomes a leading cultural ambassador of Japan and in 1986 performs a tea ceremony for the visiting Charles and Diana.

In 1988 Soshitsu paid $1.7 million in income tax. A real major leaguer, Soshitsu makes a great deal of money signing his autograph ($2,500 for writing his name on a tea bowl, for example). As *iemoto*, he also benefits from the trickling up of fees from tea students around the world. The executive staff of Soshitsu's organization comprises former high officers of the tax, police, and public prosecutor's offices. Urasenke's flamboyance annoys tea purists, but it attracts attention and keeps the students coming in.

Soshitsu, who ranks among the largest income-tax payers in Japan, makes money every time he signs his name on a tea bowl, brazier, or tea whisk.

Urasenke has two branches. The first is the tea school. The second is the Tanko Group, which controls related business enterprises, many of which feed off the tea school's membership. Tankosha, for example, is a publisher of fine art books. Kyoto Insatsu is a color printer. Tanko Sogyo manages warehouses. Sen Art Studio designs tearooms and sells tea utensils. Matsue Kosan owns hotels in Waikiki. Green International is an overseas travel agent. Another company sells airplanes. And so on. At the top of all this is Soshitsu, who arises at 5:30 every morning to chant and give thanks to his ancestors, including the great Rikyu.

Like any big business, Urasenke has diversified to create new avenues for the investment and disposition of its cash.

MATSUSHITA ELECTRIC

Konosuke Matsushita was often referred to by his countrymen as the "god of Japanese management." His obituary in the *New York Times* noted that "his flexibility was his particular genius, enabling his company to make the transitions necessary to become a major industrial enterprise." In 1988 Matsushita Electric Industrial had worldwide sales estimated at $42 billion. The Matsushita products in Japan go under the brand name National. In the 1920s Konosuke saw the word *international* in his newspaper and, not knowing what it meant (he spoke no English), looked it up in the dictionary. In so doing he came across *national*, meaning "of or relating to a people or a nation"—a perfect description for Konosuke's new company. Konosuke registered the National trademark in Japan, but when he began doing business in America he found he couldn't use the name there—it was already registered to someone else. His own name—Matsushita—was too strange to Americans. So the company began to use the name Panasonic, which had originally been used on exported hi-fi speakers and portable radios. Today the Panasonic name appears on everything from coffee pots and electric fans to refrigerators and prefab housing. Other familiar Matsushita brands are Quasar and Technics. Matsushita also owns a majority interest in

JVC. ***page 17***: Konosuke said he was drawn to the idea of making bicycle lamps from his experience as an apprentice in a bicycle shop. His own bike at the time (1923) used a candle lamp that had to be relit often, even during a short ride. Battery lamps existed, but they ran down in only two to three hours. Matsushita's new design used a 120–130 milliampere bulb instead of the standard 400–500 milliampere model, and the battery he devised would allow the lamp to burn thirty to fifty hours. Electrical parts distributors didn't want to carry the new battery lamps since they felt customers wouldn't be able to obtain replacement parts. Bike dealers looked on the lamp as a mere novelty—and unreliable. Konosuke's strategy was to develop demand at the retail level so that the big distributors would have to carry the lamp. He realized that his own company was too small to service the retailers individually, although it was to the retailers that he distributed the lamps as a promotion in the first place. ***page 23***: Over the years Konosuke developed an elaborate philosophy based on the fundamental notion that it is the unique destiny of humankind—alone among all the creatures of the earth —to think, to create, and to manage, and that it is therefore the responsibility of humans, as caretakers of the planet, to bring every other living thing to its fullest potential. Konosuke was the sponsor and recipient of numerous awards.

His PHP Institute, founded just after the war, today publishes magazines in Japanese, English, and Spanish. The institute began the Kyoto Colloquium on Global Change in 1983, based on a core group of eleven intellectuals and business leaders, to lay down fundamental principles on how the world should evolve peacefully and prosperously. As president of the Science and Technology Foundation of Japan, Konosuke helped establish the Japan Prize (Japan's version of the Nobel Prize in science and technology) in 1985. His idea about resurfacing Japan to create more land area was prompted by the oil shock and world recession of the 1970s. Another favorite idea at that time was to eliminate all taxes in Japan by creating interest-bearing funds from government budgetary surpluses that could be loaned out to individuals and foreign nations.

MITSUI GROUP

Mitsui's success parallels the success of Japan Inc. The information in this section is based largely on the fascinating book *Mitsui: Three Centuries of Japanese Business* by John G. Roberts (Tokyo: Weatherhill, 1973, 1989). Companies in the Mitsui group are involved in trading, shipbuilding, real estate, mining, oil, chemicals, and banking. Total transactions of the group in 1985 (this and other data in this section are from Roberts's book) came to $182.6 billion, "an amount equal to the gross national product of India in the same year." There are other Japanese business groups, such as Sumitomo and Mitsubishi, that are even *larger*.   **page 26**: The Mitsui were in the service of the Sasaki clan. Takayasu was officially known as the Lord of Echigo, from which title would derive the name of the retail store Echigoya later established in Edo.   **page 27**: Classes in Japan were ranked as follows: samurai, farmer, artisan, merchant. That is, tradesmen were of the lowest class, which makes Sokubei's decision all the more startling. But as the samurai, unskilled in commerce and forced to keep up their households and appearances, fell into debt, the lowly merchant gradually emerged as the central player in banking, the economy, and manufacturing, not to mention the popular arts of the day.   **page 30**: Hachirobei's shop in Nihonbashi was on the site of what is today the famous Mitsukoshi Department Store. (The character *echi* in Echigoya can also be read *koshi*.) Hachirobei pursued friendships with playwrights and poets so that the name of his store would be heard more frequently on the streets and in conversation. Among the various perquisites enjoyed by Mitsui employees in the 17th century were a fixed work week, regular breaks during the day, profit sharing, dormitory housing, and training in deportment and speech. **page 31**: Roberts suggests that

Hachirobei went after a position of official standing with the court to win friends and defenders and, just as important, to keep himself apprised of information that might affect his business. While he may have known his way around aristocratic circles, Hachirobei never forgot he was a merchant. His special interest was in money. He opened up money exchange houses in Edo, Osaka, and Kyoto, and by means of this network he could escape the commissions he had previously been paying to settle his accounts. He also devised a system of sending funds by money order between Edo and Osaka, giving himself the opportunity to use the money until payment was required. The corporate family Hachirobei created consisted of nine houses, which the eldest son, Takahira, then reorganized into a corporate-style association. Each house, or family, was managed separately but would participate jointly in certain businesses. Each family would contribute its income to the main group, which would then loan it out again to family members with interest. Incredible reserves of funds were built up in this manner. A dozen years or so before he died, Takahira issued a document that he said contained the wisdom passed down from Hachirobei. This "House Constitution" contained a number of standard clauses but also addressed matters of authority, harmony, and propriety that would make the house function better. The family members, who

were the managers of the family businesses, were exhorted to find reliable, talented people to serve as their chief clerks and managers— this would prove their salvation in later years. They were also urged to stay out of politics and to never loan money to samurai lords.   **page 32**: Rihachi's true origin is unclear. It is possible he was nearly illiterate. He was for a time a footman retainer in the service of Tadataka Oguri, whose son, Tadamasa, would become the same commissioner of finance who made such harsh demands on the Mitsui coffers. Between 1863 and 1866 the Mitsui had been forced to provide huge sums to the government. At the same time the Mitsui had also botched some of their own financing deals and were teetering on bankruptcy. Hachiroemon Kofuku, then the head of the family, probably had no choice but to give in to Rihachi's demand. As Roberts suggests, he may have blamed himself for his failure to observe the rules of the household, which urged the care and close supervision of subordinates. That Rihachi could come in and take over such a vital area of the Mitsui empire with no family connection and no employment history is extraordinary in the Japanese context. Upon his ascension, Rihachi discarded his old name and became reborn as the much nobler-sounding Rizaemon Minomura. True to his word, he was able to get the government to reduce its demand on the Mitsui treasury. The branch of business placed under Minomura's control, separate from the draper's and the retailing side, would eventually become the Mitsui Bank. From this point on, the real power and brains behind the Mitsui would reside not in the family but in their hired minions, who, it must be said, were as loyal and tenacious in pursuit of Mitsui glory as any born to the name. **page 33**: The overthrow of the Tokugawa shogunate in Edo in 1868 is called the Meiji Restoration, because it returned the Emperor Meiji from his base in Kyoto to the supreme position in the government at Edo. The city of the shogunate was renamed Tokyo, meaning "Eastern Capital." The rebel forces are said to have met with the Mitsui on numerous occasions prior to the actual campaign. Among the rebels was Kaoru Inoue. Extremely influential within the new administration, he arranged for Mitsui to handle most of the banking needs of the government (and in the course of doing so make for itself a handsome profit). In 1874 the government demanded that private holders of official funds post collateral equal to their deposits. Roberts suggests that this was part of a plan to destroy Mitsui's competition and that the Ministry of Finance, through Inoue, had signaled Mitsui its intention and given the house time to prepare adequate collateral instruments. Mitsui's competitors, who had not been forewarned, were unable to satisfy the government's demand and were

forced to restrict their activities, leaving Mitsui on top. **page 34**: The silk-reeling mill was built with imported French technology and served as a place of employment for daughters of samurai houses, who would otherwise have had no source of income. Mitsui took over operation of the mill in 1893. Using both its management skills and its long experience in the draper's business in the capital and other cities throughout Japan, Mitsui soon made the mill a profit center. By the end of the century, Japan was producing three-fourths of the world's total manufacture of raw silk.

page 35: Dan Takuma was the son of a samurai in Fukuoka. He was sent on a mission to the United States in 1871 when he was thirteen, and ended up staying there to finish his education at MIT, earning a degree in mining engineering. After he returned to Japan he was hired in 1881 to run the Miike mines. Using technological innovations, he made the mines extremely lucrative. Much of the Mitsui enterprise developed in the 20th century from the enormous profits earned by coal from the mines. Working conditions for the laborers—who included women and children—were nearly intolerable. At Omuta, another Mitsui mine, workers put in fourteen-hour days at low pay and suffered a fatality rate three times that in England. Strikes and union organizing were illegal; if convicted, one might be put in a chain gang and made to work in the mines as a convict anyway.

According to one analysis, in Kimpei Shiba and Kenzo Nozue's *What Makes Japan Tick*, the coal mine, located in Miike, was such a good source of revenue for Mitsui that the company was caught unprepared when oil-based fuels began to surpass coal in the mid-20th century. Mitsubishi, which had fought Mitsui for the control of the Miike mine, had been forced early on to make alliances with oil companies and was therefore in a much better position to fuel the postwar expansion.

page 36: Meiji Japan (post-1868) was eager to join the ranks of industrialized nations and eliminate the inequities in its dealings with Western colonial powers. The personal relationships from which international business and technology exchanges developed generally involved Western-style entertaining, speaking English, and a degree of conviviality that many Japanese were not used to. The best parties in Tokyo were held at Baron Mitsui's estate, with its extensive acreage and Japo-European-style mansion. Within the Japanese peerage were about a thousand family heads consisting of members of the old imperial aristocracy and samurai who had led the revolt against the shogunate, plus distinguished merchants and other commoners who had helped the cause. Having been born a merchant (although of ex-samurai stock), Baron Mitsui was among the low ranks of the peerage. He contrived to work his family's way up into the higher ranks through judicious choice of marriage partners. Over the years, the Mitsui became intertwined with the imperial family, the priesthood, and powerful figures of government, as well as other industrialist and merchant families. **page 37**: Roberts notes that Japanese manufacturers could import lumber from North America and then export it as plywood to the east coast of the U.S. for $56.50 per 1,000 board feet, whereas American producers were selling their plywood for $137.50 on the west coast, where it was made. Mitsui's trade in machinery and manufacturing equipment was one of the primary agents for Japan's industrial growth in this century. Mitsui handled 40% of Japan's machinery exports, made exclusive trading arrangements with foreign companies like Pratt and Whitney and Bristol Aeroplane, and established joint ventures in Japan with firms like General Electric (an early stockholder in Toshiba) and Otis Elevator. **page 38**: The term *zaibatsu* for commercial enterprises like the House of Mitsui is no longer used in Japan, except by critics of big business who wish to link modern-day corporate greed to prewar exploitation and profiteering. The term for affiliated industrial groupings today is *keiretsu*. Control of Mitsui at this time was firmly in the hands of the *obanto*, the brilliant outsiders who served as business managers and chief executives of the family's various enterprises. The Mitsui family members were primarily figureheads who spent their days squabbling with each other and enjoying their wealth. They were nevertheless valuable for their political and hereditary connections, which they continued (and continue) to exercise. In 1933 Seihin Ikeda of Mitsui Bank was made the head of the Mitsui enterprise group. Ikeda was able to persuade the family heads to remove themselves from their managerial posts on the pretext that being less visible would reduce the risk of terrorist assassination. Ikeda also established a philanthropic foundation in Mitsui's name like those set up by Rockefeller and Carnegie in the United States, and for much the same reason—to deflect public resentment against such an enormous concentration of wealth and power in the hands of a single enterprise.

page 39: In the years before the war, Roberts estimates that one out of every ten Japanese depended on a Mitsui enterprise or subsidiary for his wages. By 1945 Mitsui was possibly the largest business organization in the world. The total number of companies estimated to be under Mitsui control was 336. Mitsui may have protested to the Occupation authorities that it had made no money from the war, but records show that paid-up capital of the zaibatsu during the war years increased more than 4 times, versus 1.8 for that of other Japanese businesses. Just before the war ended,

the zaibatsu arranged for the government to nationalize the munitions factories and to reimburse industry for any debts incurred. The result of this stratagem was that even in August 1946, a year after Japan's surrender, the zaibatsu were still gobbling up funds from the treasury that might otherwise have gone to public assistance and recovery. **page 40**: The reason Mitsui suffered more under the disintegration of the zaibatsu than other enterprises is that it had been such a successful money machine in the prewar years. With less debt and lots of cash, it was not in a position to write off nonreceivables and thus had to forfeit a higher percentage of its holdings. Mitsui was also forced to give up many of its neighborhood bank branches. The legacy of this can be seen in Mitsui Bank's recent merger with the strong retailer Taiyo Kobe Bank to form the world's second-largest bank with some $371 billion in assets. **page 41**: Richard Nixon visited Japan several times in the 1960s on behalf of his clients, who included Pepsico and the U.S. branch of Mitsui. Nixon was well connected with the banking and industrial establishment in the U.S., which profited handsomely in its business dealings in Asia (and Japan) as the Vietnam War expanded.

page 42: The Chemical Bank/Bache loan was important because it set a precedent for foreign investment in postwar companies. The assistance American companies provided to

Japanese firms in which they had previously held stock gave these ex-zaibatsu companies a competitive advantage against other firms that had lacked previous connections overseas.   **pages 44–45**: The number of companies within the Mitsui Group is now, by Roberts's count, about 120. Executives of these various companies convene at regularly scheduled meetings to discuss general business. Think tanks have been set up to study information networks, electronic banking, and emergent technologies. There is also a council of Mitsui firms whose purpose is to figure out ways of fixing up group companies in decline, such as in the mining and shipbuilding industries. Despite all this interconnection, Mitsui Bussan, the trading company, relies on the group for only 12 to 13% of its business, half of what Mitsubishi's and Sumitomo's trading companies derive from their groups. The several enterprise groups in Japan, while they remain competitive, now co-invest in projects that no single group is willing to handle alone. The American Occupation intended to break up the zaibatsu and develop the spirit of individualism among entrepreneurs in Japan. But it was a bit like breaking up globs of mercury. The separate entities soon reformed, not simply because it made business sense but because the Japanese organization is primarily communal and operates best when the human network is thick and overgrown with obligation,

commitment, tradition, and blind loyalty. Yet business is changing in Japan, and the old groupings are giving way to new alliances formed by new, Western-style methods, such as the above-mentioned merger of the Mitsui and Taiyo Kobe banks.

MORI BUILDING

Go up to the top of Tokyo Tower in downtown Tokyo and look out toward the northeast. In the nearby business areas of Toranomon and Shinbashi, where real estate developer Taikichiro Mori grew up, you will see Mori's buildings. The top of each one has a huge sign with Mori's name followed by a number. Just as Japanese children often given their sons names indicating their order of birth—Ichiro = first (*ichi* means "one"), Jiro = second (*ji* means "next") and so on—Mori has given his concrete progeny a rank in the Mori family. And that's how he says he thinks of them—as his children.   **page 48**: The Ginza Hachikan Shrine is 300 years old. The ground floor and floor 2 form a prayer hall. Floors 3 to 5 are rented out to bars and clubs. Floor 6 is a health center and floor 7 is a hall for ceremonies. The deity (*kami*) is housed on floor 8. The national Shinto organization was critical of this arrangement, saying that the *kami* must always be in contact with the ground. The head priest of Hachikan Shrine got around this by installing an earth-filled forty-foot pipe from floor 8 to ground level.

page 49: The banks have been especially embarrassed in the past few years by having their connections to strong-arm real estate operations disclosed in the press. Galloping real estate values have helped create what is called the "New Poor" in Japan. A whole class of people, who at one time had aspired to home ownership, must now give up their dream or suffer long commutes to ticky-tacky neighborhoods in the faraway suburbs. The government, fearing a new consumer movement and worried that too much dissatisfaction over land prices could push things to a breaking point, has been accused of willfully underappraising real estate values in Tokyo.

page 50: Mori's father believed that the landlord and tenant constitute one large family. He would help tenants settle disputes and find work. He would lower the rent if a son or husband went off to war. He would help with schooling costs if the parents couldn't afford it. His father's generosity surely helped shape the young Taikichiro's own ideals. An additional factor may have been Taikichiro's experience at university, where he heard much criticism from his fellow students, many of them socialists, about the exploitation of the workers by the rich. When the earthquake struck in 1923, Mori was a student at Tokyo Commercial College. For a while he worked at Mitsui, where he learned about real estate development from the chairman himself. He did not actually begin building until he was fifty-five years old. Mori quit his university job—he was a professor of economics at Yokohama City University—to concentrate on real estate in 1959. *page 52*: Mori also gives lectures, which are transcribed into books for employees. The subject matter is not so much the ins and outs of the real estate business but Mori's own ruminations on Japan and modern progress. *page 53*: The government provided some development funds, but the project could not have succeeded without Mori's patient leadership and local ties. In the end, of all the landowners in the area, only fifty-seven decided to cooperate. The rest left and got Mori's assistance in finding new land and housing. The ones who stayed received rent-free apartments and limited property rights. One man who used to own a sushi restaurant in the area now runs an ice cream store within Ark Hills. Another man, once the local butcher, now operates a delicatessen.

page 54: Mori's office explains that the strategically located Ark Hills gets its name from "Akasaka–Roppongi–Knot." Akasaka is an area of expensive clubs, hotels, and restaurants near the locus of political power in Kasumigaseki. Roppongi is a bustling nightclub district. Adjacent to the Ark Hills site are the famous Hotel Okura, the American Embassy, the Spanish Embassy, the headquarters of Japan IBM, and the huge Akasaka Twin Tower office complex. The Ark Mori

Building has air conditioning that can create separate microenvironments throughout and computers that control everything from the electrical system to disaster contingencies. One of the reasons the office building filled up so quickly is the shortage of space in downtown Tokyo. In 1986, Tokyo had an office vacancy rate of only 0.2% compared with 5% in Manhattan.

page 55: In his mid-seventies, Mori had a heart attack and slowed down. He began wearing a kimono every day. Mori doesn't drink, smoke, or pursue any hobbies. Deadly serious most of the time, when asked to sing he will perform Schubert songs in German.

TOKYO DISNEYLAND

Mitsui and Keisei guaranteed a loan of $1.5 billion borrowed from a syndicate of twenty-two banks. Oriental Land's holdings, valued at about $650 per square foot, today have a total worth of over 1,600 times their original value.

page 58: Oriental Land became embroiled in a political scandal surrounding the Urayasu development. Mitsui board members had close connections with the ruling Liberal Democratic Party, and there were reports that money had passed hands in an attempt to change the restrictions on usage for the land-filled area. Keisei Electric Railway owns 52% of Oriental Land, and Mitsui owns 48%. But Mitsui, with its vast political and economic influence, is by far the stronger partner.   *page 60*: Each negotiating session alternated between countries. Ron Cayo was a lawyer. Frank Stanek, the other Disney negotiator, was with the Imagineering group, the Disney department that conceives and designs attractions. The Japanese media, in addition to being skeptical about Mitsui's real motivations, were unanimous in predicting the project's failure. Hajime Tsuboi, president of Mitsui Real Estate at the time, himself said, "Tokyo Disneyland's particular character as an enterprise is that it is next to impossible for us to make it profitable."   *page 62*: Before the agreement was made with Disney, the Ministry of Finance had set the maximum duration of a foreign rights licensing agreement in Japan at twenty years. Disney wanted a fifty-year deal and won in the end, settling for forty-five years. Currently eight Disney advisors work fulltime in Japan giving advice on entertainment, design, upkeep, merchandising, food, and employee relations.   *page 63*: Captain Eo and Big Thunder Mountain were added in 1988. Over the next five years, three new major attractions are planned. Almost 70% of the guests each day are repeaters, so the park must constantly come up with new rides. Among the many employees at Disneyland are a host of real-live Americans, who, along with the food and signboards, make the Japanese visitors feel they have truly spent a day in a magical kingdom—the United States. Oriental Land is now discussing opening a second park on the Urayasu site. This will be a studio tour. The company says, "We would like to build it by ourselves, but projects constructed solely by Japanese often turn out to be somewhat uninteresting." MCA Enterprises signed a deal with Nippon Steel in 1987 to bring its own Universal Studio Tour theme park to Japan. This is a good example of how aging Japanese industries with vast land holdings are pushing aggressively into the burgeoning leisure-time market in Japan.

NISSIN FOODS

Ramen noodles are made with wheat flour and, unlike Italian pasta, contain no egg. The noodles are eaten in a flavored broth with bean sprouts, pieces of chicken, corn, fish, or whatever the chef feels like adding. Ando's first instant noodle product was packaged in plastic bags. The consumer would remove the preseasoned noodles from the bag and put them, together with other ingredients, in a saucepan at home. Ando's great invention, Cup Noodle, was a complete "meal" served in a styrofoam container. Seasonings and freeze-dried meats and vegetables were enclosed in a sealed aluminum pouch. Officially, Cup Noodle is classified as a snack food. In the 1970s, so many college students were depending on Cup Noodle for their entire food intake

that there was real concern about malnutrition and vitamin deficiency among Japanese youth.   **page 66**: By Japanese law, nationality follows bloodline. Ando, born in Taiwan of Japanese parents, was considered a Japanese citizen.   **page 68**: Ando's version of the black-marketing charges is as follows. Ando's factory made airplane starters. One day Ando noticed a discrepancy between the materials inventory and the goods shipped. Suspecting theft, Ando went to the police, who sent him to the military police. The MPs turned on Ando and accused him of covering up for someone else. Later Ando found out that one of his employees had a friend in the military police. The military was outside the law, and torture during interrogation was not unusual. In prison Ando was beaten and repeatedly kicked in the stomach. He became very ill. His own connections among the military finally secured his release. Out of jail, Ando was hospitalized for sixty-five days. He has had stomach problems ever since. **page 69**: Ando estimates that his postwar ¥40 million in today's money would be worth about $750 million.   **page 72**: Many Japanese resented Ando's close connections with the Americans. Ando's translator, a man named Ozawa, was especially good at greasing the wheels and using the American Occupation forces to sidestep the Japanese police authorities. Ando was given a choice: four years hard labor or leave the country. Ando chose to go to prison. Charges were eventually dropped and Ando was freed, but he was never compensated for all the property that had been seized and disposed of.   **page 73**: Now bankrupt, Ando can afford to become a Japanese again and switches his citizenship.   **page 74**: Ando was looking for something to mass-produce. To succeed, Ando realized that a food product had to be (1) tasty, (2) something addictive, like Coca Cola, (3) capable of being preserved and thus kept around the house at all times, like rice, (4) easy to make in little time, (5) inexpensive, and (6) safe and nutritious. To make the product "instant," Ando decided he had to build the flavoring into the noodle. But whenever he tried adding flavored broth to the dough, the noodles would either crumble or stick to the machine. Finally Ando realized that the salt in the flavoring was affecting the gluten in the flour. Water content was another problem. When the noodle was fried prior to packaging, the water would escape and leave a bubble in the noodle. The size of the bubble determined the consistency of the noodle when it was reconstituted with hot water.   **page 75**: Ando designed the first manufacturing facility himself and made his own wire basket for frying. After putting the noodles in cellophane bags, he took them to the wholesale market. At ¥35 per bag, the product was expensive. Wanting to be paid in cash was unusual. Standard terms in Japan were 90 to 120

days. Ando's second factory was constructed on a twenty-four-hour schedule. He moved equipment into the factory and began production before the building was finished.

page 77: Ando spent a great deal of time experimenting with different shapes for his Cup Noodle container. It had to be a shape that wouldn't spill and wouldn't slip out of the hand. And it had to have that ineffable quality of consumer appeal. Styrofoam was the perfect material, because it was insulating and lightweight. But it was a relatively new material, and Japanese manufacturing methods were quite primitive at the time. Ando's first Japanese-made cups would break or the hot water would leak out. Claims of burned hands came to Nissin. Tying up with Dart brought quality control to the cups, but there was a problem with the way the cups smelled. Ando discovered that he could remove the smell by heating the cups after they were manufactured. This technique was later emulated by manufacturers around the world.   **page 78**: Until recently, it was considered bad manners to eat while walking on the street in Japan. Japanese ice cream stores in particular had to overcome this prejudice before they could be successful.   **page 79**: Ando frequently ignores orthodox market research, but he does like to take his case "to the people" to let them decide. Ando figured that if the market didn't exist in America he could always take the machinery back to Japan for use there. (The Japanese eat ten times as much ramen each year as Americans do.) Ando picked four markets in Los Angeles and went there himself, dressed all in white, to give personal demonstrations. Ando's concern about Americans slurping their noodles may have been over-cautious. He did discover, however, that if he made the noodles short enough and a little flatter, most people could get them into their mouths without having to slurp them up noisily between their lips. Nissin now has between 60 and 70% of the American Oriental noodle market. Nissin has offices in Singapore, Hong Kong, and Brazil and manufactures locally in ten countries. It recently purchased an equity interest in an Indian company that makes freeze-dried shrimps and spices. **page 81**: Rice is more than just a food in Japan. Many Japanese see it as a sacred element of their national heritage. It is commonly used as an offering to the indigenous Shinto gods. By making it "instant," Ando may have offended many traditionalists, who see the harvesting of rice and the ritual eating of it during each meal as sacrosanct. Ando's first son, Nissin's ex-president, now works in the natural foods industry in Osaka. By all accounts, he was much too cautious for his freewheeling father. The Foodeum building in Tokyo was the brainchild of Nissin's new president, Ando's second son, Koki. The building, in addition to its disco,

restaurants, and cafe, has a test kitchen and presents lectures on food every week. The corporate offices are on floors 4 to 11. Most company headquarters in Japan are located in business districts. By putting Nissin's smack in the middle of an entertainment area, the company was declaring the importance of high visibility and customer relations. Flexibility in the face of fast-changing food trends is also crucial: the company's annual report notes that Nissin has just launched a successful new product called Ramen-ya, which is a line of *refrigerated* and *fresh* wet noodles.

FOX BAGELS

Legend has it that the bagel was invented in Austria. It was the Austrian Jews who brought the bagel to New York. Today, the United States is the leading bagel-producing country in the world. In Japan, the bagel has no more ethnic identity than a donut. Setting up a business in Japan is not easy if you're a foreigner. Lyle had trouble borrowing money at first—he was turned down seven times until he met the Japanese trading company with the American bagel-lover on its staff (see page 89). One reason foreigners have a hard time is that Japanese lenders know how difficult and time-consuming it is for foreigners (or anyone for that matter) to establish the human relationships with suppliers and customers that are the cornerstone of business in Japan.

Lyle for example, must go regularly to the department stores that sell his bagels just to sit down and talk face to face with the managers there. On the other hand, a foreigner doing business in Japan has considerable flexibility, since he can choose, depending on the situation, to take either the patient Eastern or aggressive Western (pigheaded tough negotiator) approach. It's also easier for a foreigner to make appointments without the customary networks of introductions. When Lyle wanted to see the president of McDonald's Japan, for example, he sent a letter and the president's secretary called *him*.   *page 86*: It is not so strange to meet Russians in Japan. Called White Russians, these people are descendants of refugees from the 1917 October Revolution who fled to Japan by way of China. *page 88*: Lyle did not exactly tell the truth to the North Carolinian. Thinking that the man would want money for his recipe, Lyle wrote to him and said he needed to know how to make bagels because he wanted to make them now and then for the foreign Jewish community in Tokyo. It turned out that the rice flour was used only to dust the bagels so they wouldn't stick as they baked. Lyle's experience with the suppliers of his ingredients was quite typical of Japan. Lyle was small, inexperienced, and low on cash, but the suppliers figured that the time they spent investing on building up his business and know-how might return to them at a later date. Lyle still buys his flour for baking from the same supplier who first sold it to him.   *page 89*: Selling to the foreign-market-oriented National Azabu store was fine, but it was his success at Seibu's Shibuya store that really established Lyle as a legitimate retailer in Japanese eyes. Department stores rent out stalls in their basements to various food retailers and take 20 to 22% of gross in lieu of rent. Lyle moved his factory and retail shop to Roppongi, a fashionable eating and entertainment district close to where lots of foreigners work and live. The deal Lyle arranged allowed him to "lease" everything, including the painting of the walls in the shop! The trading company that loaned Lyle the money took 5% of sales every month for the period of the lease.   *page 90*: Lyle's Roppongi location was only 700 square feet. When he subcontracted out the baking the first time, he gave the bakery his recipe, leased it his equipment, taught the Japanese bakers how to make bagels, and forbid them to divulge the recipe or make bagels for anyone else. Lyle liked the arrangement, but it cut into his profitability by raising his costs 50%. The baker got fed up because bagels are so difficult to make well—they have to be boiled in water just before they're baked, and the proofing of the dough has to be exactly right. This is why Lyle thought Pasco (see page 92) would never be able to make bagels as good as his—they're just too delicate for a large commercial bakery. **page 91**: To compare: the favorite varieties among Lyle's foreign customers are onion, poppy, and whole wheat, in that order. About 90% of Lyle's customers are now Japanese. **page 92**: Pasco also operates a bakery in Los Angeles. Pasco's spies would come into Lyle's Roppongi shop, order plain bagels, and pull them apart at the counter, discussing their texture and quality right in front of Lyle. Then they would ask for a receipt for their purchase—made out to Pasco. Generally matters are carried out a bit more discreetly in Japan, and Lyle thinks that maybe Pasco was trying to intimidate him. The machine Pasco ordered was a smaller version of the one Lyle had. Lyle knew it backward and forward since his own machine had been shipped to him in pieces and he had had to put it together himself. Believing that more competition can only stimulate the market, Lyle is now trying to help an American bagel manufacturer find a joint venture partner in Japan. The Japanese, particularly those outside the big cities, are still not very bagelwise. **page 93**: Wall Street Sandwiches was originally set up as an independent company with Lyle, a friend, and a few investors. The partners spent four months testing the market, developing the menu, and contacting suppliers. In August 1988 Wall Street Sandwiches and Fox Bagels merged, with Lyle giving up a small percentage of his bagel company in return for a majority interest in Wall Street. In addition to the original sandwich shop, across the street from the Ark Hills development, there is now a second sandwich shop in the back of Lyle's bagel shop in Roppongi. Both shops service different territories around the city. All deliveries are made by motor scooter within two hours. The American businessmen make the worst customers— always requesting substitutions on their sandwiches and being very picky about every detail, just as if they were still in New York.

SHISEIDO

Shiseido was radically reorganized in 1988. There are some 25,000 Shiseido chain stores in Japan, and the parent company had been coercing them to buy products to strengthen its bottom line. By halting the practice, Shiseido suddenly had too much extra inventory that, because of rapidly shifting fashions in the cosmetics industry, it was unable to sell. Profits fell 50% as a result. Even so, Shiseido paid out its annual dividend to shareholders. **page 98**: Shiseido's toothpaste, introduced in 1888 and the first in Japan, was called Fukuhara Sanitary Tooth Paste. Yushin later left the management of the pharmacy to his wife to go off and establish what is now the second-oldest life insurance company in Japan—Asahi Seimei. It was to observe the insurance business that Yushin went to Europe in 1900. When Yushin began Japan's first soda fountain in his Ginza pharmacy in 1902, everything, from the ice cream manufacturing equipment to the straws, had to be imported by sea. **page 100**: Shinzo's photographs of Europe were gathered into a book in 1922, *Paris et la Seine*, which was well received. **page 101**: In 1916 Shinzo started up Shiseido's cosmetics department right next door to the Ginza pharmacy. Shinzo selected the camellia for the company image for three reasons: (1) it was a favorite among Japanese people, (2) it was regarded as the best garden flower in the United States, and (3) it was used in the manufacture of cosmetics. Sue Yabe was Shiseido's first design director. A fan of Beardsley and Erté, he was instrumental in setting the art nouveau style for Shiseido's graphic works. Shiseido's advertising, over the first few decades at least, was fresh by Japanese standards but largely derivative of French and European designs. It did, however, help familiarize the Japanese with Western graphic design and has helped create a stylistic reservoir from which modern-day Japanese designers still draw for inspiration. **page 102**: Shinzo had a network of many famous talents—people like Ryuzaburo Umehara, a painter, and Toyoo Iwata, a novelist—on whom he relied for the latest news of music, art, and fashion in Paris. Much of the information was used to develop new designs and styles, but it was also disseminated to the public by way of *Hanatsubaki*. Somewhat akin to a Japanese *Vogue* or *Harper's Bazaar*, *Hanatsubaki* was one of the few Japanese magazines in the 1930s not to be infected by wartime militarism. **page 103**: Shiseido lost numerous employees during the war. Some left the company, while others were sent off to battle. At the end of the war, Shiseido welcomed anyone who wanted to come back—and it maintains the same welcome-home policy toward ex-employees today. In 1949 the company was listed on the Tokyo Stock Exchange. A stock sharing plan has made employees the second-largest Shiseido shareholder. **page 104**: In 1983 Shiseido became the first cosmetics company to have a technology cooperation agreement with China. Shiseido products are marketed in China under the name Hua Zi. In 1986 Carita S.A. with its salons and beautician schools in France became a member of the Shiseido group. In Japan there is now the Shiseido-owned Carita beauty salon, designed by Andrée Putman to look like the inside of a luxury cabin cruiser. Shiseido has also begun a joint venture with Pierre Fabre S.A., a French pharmaceutical group. **page 105**: Shiseido puts out 700 new products a year, but many of these merely represent new colors or packaging schemes for existing lines.

FOLIO

The life of the model in Japan, while lucrative and glamorous, is not easy. Many of the girls come from middle-class backgrounds that just haven't prepared them for life in the big city, much less the big, booming, busy city of Tokyo. As nonliterate, nonspeaking, female temporary workers, they are in many Japanese eyes just above dogs in status. The government puts them in the same visa class as bar hostesses and entertainers.   **page 108**: Hiroshi Aoyagi was born in 1941. How could a melon cost $80? In Japan, "gift" melons are sold in elaborately wrapped wooden boxes. The idea is not so much what's in the box—it is a good melon, after all—but how much it costs (that is, how much of the donor's debt to the donee will it pay off).   **page 111**: Folio has a staff of twenty-four and at any one time thirty Japanese and fifty foreign models are on call. The foreign models generally stay one or two months. They are carefully screened before being invited to Japan to work. Folio reps go abroad six times a year in search of new faces that suit the fast-changing fashion trends in Japan.   **page 112**: Folio has also begun a joint agency with the Elite model agency, called Elite-Folio. This takes advantage of Elite's huge syndicate by allowing Folio to tap into Elite's talent bank at its agencies throughout the world.
page 113: The studios are essentially empty houses and are always designed in impeccable architectural taste. They can also be rented out for private parties and to designers for fashion shows. Two country studios are in Kawasaki, near the beach, and in Hakone, in the mountains southwest of Tokyo. (Designed for privacy, they are often used for nude photography.) The Hakone studio has a sauna as well as a traditional Japanese tatami room.

DENTSU

According to the trade magazine *Ad Age*, Dentsu is the number one advertising agency in the world in terms of billings and profits. The company's billings in 1988 totaled $7.3 billion. Pretax profit in 1987 was $884.5 million. Dentsu has a total of 5,800 employees in twenty-seven offices in Japan and twenty agencies overseas. It handles 23% of Japan's total advertising, twice as much as that of its closest competitor, Hakuhodo.   **page 116**: Mitsunaga's two companies were Nippon Kokoku K.K. (Japan Advertising Corporation) and Denpo Tsushin-sha (Telegraph News Agency). Mitsunaga sought investors, but the economy was in a bad state at the end of the war, and few people thought a news agency could be profitable. Japan Advertising had competition from other ad agencies, which as a group tried to impede its business. Mitsunaga offered low commissions and honest dealings, and gradually his company won the trust of advertisers and newspapers alike. The news wire service was ahead of its time in providing cultural and economic news as well as hard news, and its reports of Japan's stunning victory in the Russo-Japanese War in 1906 gave the company an added boost.

page 117: By 1910 Dentsu had bureaus in eight major cities and fifty-four correspondents throughout Japan.   **page 118**: After consolidation, Dentsu controlled advertising agencies in Tokyo, Osaka, Nagoya, and Kyushu.   **page 119**: Like most other successful Japanese business leaders, Mitsunaga understood the importance of human relationships. It was he who began the tradition of the Dentsu New Year's party as a means of bringing together company executives and leading Japanese politicians, business persons, and artists. In 1988 the party attracted over 10,000 people and cost a total of $3.7 million.

page 120: According to Kimpei Shiba and Kenzo Nozue's book, *What Makes Japan Tick*, from which some of this Dentsu information was taken, had Hoshiro Mitsunaga still been alive (he died in 1945) he would never have accepted the Domei stock transfer. But Dentsu was preoccupied, for its own chief executive had been forced to step down by the Occupation, and the deal was allowed to go through. The ex-president of Domei was named Inosuke Furuno; he had resigned from the news agency to help in the creation of Kyodo, but he

himself did not hold any position at Kyodo. His problem was that the law forbid the transfer of assets and management from a liquidated company to another firm. Furuno got around this technical obstacle by calling the transfer of stock from Domei to Kyodo a "gift."

page 122: Obviously Dentsu can't control every communication medium. Yoshida's story is told in a "Corporate Comic" book published in 1988 called *Dentsu*, with the reading line "The media monster Dentsu that pulls Japan's strings— closing in on its secret citadel of energy and raw ambition." Comics about companies are a popular form of information transmission in Japan, where the literacy rate approaches 100%. The comic comes with an impressive list of bibliographical references. It notes in a sidebar that "Demon" Yoshida, after graduating from Tokyo Imperial University, applied for jobs at leading newspapers, Mitsui Bussan, Ajinomoto, and Lion Toothpaste before finally being accepted at the then-obscure ad agency Dentsu. After taking over the company, Yoshida worked to modernize its corporate structure and created separate creative and account service departments.

page 123: The story about the high-tech firms appears in the aforementioned corporate comic. Another story told in its pages concerns a small high-tech firm, a client of Dentsu's, that is manipulated into merging with a larger firm, also a

Dentsu client. Dentsu leaks word of financial improprieties on the part of the smaller company to a newsweekly. Put on the defensive, the smaller company agrees to be taken over. In the end everyone wins, because the larger company increases its market share and the smaller company gets better funding and exposure for its technology. Journalists in Japan refer to Dentsu as the "Shadow CIA." Dentsu is also known as one of the easier job placements for the wayward sons of corporate executives, who then give the agency their business.

page 124: Many people used the national railways (then called JNR) to get to the Osaka Expo, but when the event was over JNR needed a means of keeping ridership up. It turned to Dentsu, which came up with the enormously successful campaign called "Discover Japan," with the suggestive subtitle "Japan the Beautiful and Myself" (taken from the title of writer Yasunari Kawabata's 1968 Nobel Prize acceptance speech). The campaign caught perfectly Japan's growing affluence and the national mood of self-satisfaction that allowed the Japanese to let up a bit from the torrid pace of postwar recovery and revel in their own national spirit and tradition. The magazine *Business Tokyo* in September 1988 noted that Dentsu is either an investor or partner in a hundred companies working in advanced forms of communication, among them satellite broadcasting, electronic press cutting, cable TV,

digital communications, and sports marketing. In so doing Dentsu remains at the leading edge of emerging technologies, which it can then exploit in its promotional ventures. *Business Tokyo* also cites the example of the animated film *Laputa*, which Dentsu produced and later used to launch a new soft drink by Ajinomoto. Dentsu also had a hit with its movie *Dun-Huang*. It sold sponsorship of the movie to Matsushita, which used the film to promote its entry into the China market. Actors in the film also appeared in advertising for cosmetic maker Shiseido, a Dentsu client. The Tsukuba Expo of 1985 was a classic Dentsu promotional event. The real agenda of the expo was the promotion of science and technology to Japanese children, who would be the engineers, scientists, and mathematicians of the future. The expo was held in a region north of Tokyo that was being developed as a giant think tank with many research institutions and a large university. Dentsu helped the government draw up the master plan for the expo. The government's role was to oversee, but it was Dentsu that handled the details. Of the two dozen corporate pavilions, Dentsu was responsible for designing, building, staffing, and furnishing most of them. Tsukuba Expo was a great success. The name of Dentsu was barely visible on the expo site itself, but to those in the know the mark of Dentsu could be seen everywhere.

page 125: To avoid conflict, Dentsu

tries to handle different product lines of competing companies (the small car line of one automaker, the luxury line of another, for example). *Business Tokyo* makes the point that because workers don't change companies in Japan or even move between divisions at Dentsu, there is little danger of information on one client's campaign leaking to the account representative of another's. The many freelancers Dentsu hires, however, may be a threat to this security. The Hakuhodo agency is slowly gaining ground on Dentsu, although Dentsu still controls 19% of all newspaper advertising and 31% of all TV advertising in Japan, including 40% of all prime-time TV advertising in Tokyo. Dentsu's slogan is "Communications Excellence."

MUJIRUSHI RYOHIN

Just as an American lover of Japanese dress would never think of buying a kimono designed and made in Hackensack, New Jersey, until recently Japanese consumers regarded many of their own "Western-style" goods with some suspicion. Western goods were fashionable in Japan before the war. After the war they were hard to obtain and very expensive. Japanese manufacturers were not yet back on their feet. It is no wonder that the Japanese—lovers of tradition and insecure when it comes to making individual determinations of taste—became so devoted to foreign goods

from old European manufacturers as soon as they had the money to afford them. They would flaunt this devotion by selecting garments or accessories with an abundance of obvious designer logos—on their cufflinks, belts, breast pockets, neckties, socks, shoes, and even underwear. In the 1970s, many Japanese became embarrassed by this slavish devotion to foreign goods. Basic counterculture reformism was introduced into Japan from the U.S. in the 1970s, making it possible for a concept like MR to take root. In MR can also be seen a more traditional Japanese fondness for the simple and honest values of the woodworker or the potter. That the 1960s-style natural food fad came and went in Japan, while MR remains a strong marketing concept, points to an area of the Japanese psyche that is worth examining by any would-be exporter of American-made goods.   *page 129*: The Seibu organization, now called the Saison Group, is a huge merchandising force in Japan. Seiyu, part of the group, is a chain of department stores (usually with a supermarket in the basement) selling daily-life goods to mostly suburban shoppers. Seiyu wanted its new house brand to have strong recognition value among consumers. But it did not want to spend a lot of money advertising and competing with existing national brands. For its concept development director, Seiyu chose Ikko Tanaka, a high-profile art director and graphic designer. The woman who discovered the generic beer can in America was Kazuko Koike, an influential producer and consultant with ties to the fashion and art worlds. **page 130**: The kind of cotton favored in Japan was tightly woven, strong, and smooth. MR designers found that Peruvian cotton, though it lacked those qualities, was light and warm. Today MR uses thirty tons of Peruvian cotton a year for sweat suits, polo shirts, and T-shirts. Other companies in Japan have started to use it as well. Another slogan used by MR is "Salmon is the whole fish." The big hits of MR's third series of products released in 1981 were panty hose, unbleached socks, and memo pads. By October 1983, MR was into its seventh series and had developed 721 products (475 household-use items, 124 foods, 122 articles of clothing). **page 131**: Three characteristics looked for in an MR product are (1) good quality at a good price, (2) solid intrinsic value as a functional object, and (3) consideration for the consumer in terms of choice of materials, elimination of unnecessary waste and manufacturing costs, and simple packaging that is honest and informative. **page 133**: MR has spawned numerous imitators, among them Daiei Corp., whose "generic" line similarly uses four Sino-Japanese characters and plain beige packaging. Character and image are at the heart of MR's success. The problem is that MR can't grow vertically. It can't upgrade its products or allow

them to cost more without tarnishing the ideology of simple, cheap, natural. Instead, MR must grow horizontally, creating ever more items in the same price and image niche. Production and inventory management become more difficult. As the mushroom-fragment example suggests, there is a complex irony here, somewhat akin to the plight of the small neighborhood restaurant that suddenly becomes a success, moves to larger quarters, and immediately loses its *je ne sais quoi*. MR managers know exactly what their *quoi* is—whether they can hold onto it and keep the flavor is another matter. Already many consumers complain that MR products are overpriced and of only average quality. The problem may get worse, since MR says it expects by 1994 to have opened fifty new outlets and to be doing $425 million in sales per year.

URASENKE

Just as the Mitsui commercial empire has given shape to the development of the modern-day Japanese industrial economy, so have Urasenke and the tea ceremony played an influential role in the development of the modern-day Japanese aesthetic. Tea as a refined and ceremonial art—it is called *chanoyu* or *sado*, the "Way of Tea," which identifies it as being partly a spiritual form of training—is still widely practiced, of course, but more visible in Japan is the use of the trappings of tea by advertisers, architects, and fashion designers as a means of manipulating the cognitive functions of Japanese consumers. In the aesthetic pantheon, tea taste in Japan occupies roughly the same position that the Greek ideals of beauty and perfection do in the West. But if the commercially exploited tea taste has any equivalent sensibility in America, it is perhaps the refined Waspish style of Ralph Lauren, with perfect people in perfect places acting just perfect. The difference here is that tea strikes a resonant chord among all Japanese, while the Lauren look is unabashedly elitist. **page 136**: Tea from China was drunk in Japan as early as the Nara period (710–94). The tea plant itself was introduced in about 1200 by Eisai, a Zen priest. By the 15th century, tea was being drunk in a type of ceremony that relied to some extent on the connoisseurship of Chinese *objets*. This early ceremony was held in a large room. The tea was prepared elsewhere. It was Shuko who developed the idea of making the tea in front of the guests in a small and modest hut. **page 137**: Rikyu extended Shuko's simple tastes and made them more astringent. He favored an even smaller tearoom and preferred to place all the utensils directly on the floor while they were being used. The scholar H. Paul Varley cites a passage wherein Rikyu is quoted as saying, "The ceremony performed in a plain hut is an ascetic discipline, based on the Buddhist law, that is aimed at achieving spiritual salvation. To be concerned about the quality of the dwelling in which you serve tea or the flavor of the food served with it is to emphasize the mundane." **page 138**: The type of tea practiced by Hideyoshi and the other warriors of his day retained characteristics of the early tea ceremony that had been practiced in a large room. One of the great tea events of all time took place at Kitano Shrine in Kyoto in October of 1587. Hideyoshi had just conquered Kyushu. He sent out placards announcing a tea party to which all were bidden to come, even those bringing just the poor man's brew of roasted rice tea and a kettle. Some 800 tea huts filled the pine groves on the shrine grounds, and Hideyoshi, Rikyu, and two other tea masters personally served some 803 guests. **page 139**: Sen no Rikyu is probably the most important person in the entire history of Japanese aesthetics, and numerous anecdotes have grown up around his person. Among them is the famous morning glory story. Hideyoshi had heard that Rikyu's garden was full of the most beautiful morning glories. He asked Rikyu whether he could come see them, and Rikyu invited him for an early morning tea. On the appointed day, when the warlord entered Rikyu's garden, he was horrified to discover that Rikyu had cut down and removed every last blossom. Enraged, Hideyoshi entered the teahouse. There he discovered a single morning glory that the tea master had saved and placed in a vase. Hideyoshi immediately recognized how perfectly Rikyu had captured the beauty of the flower. **page 141**: Sotan was fourteen years old when his grandfather was forced to kill himself. Sotan as much as possible avoided the warriors and devoted himself to establishing tea among commoners, although he did teach some poor palace aristocrats who lacked the money to pay him. Sotan's second son, Soshu, began the Mushanokojisenke school. Sosa, his third son, and the most refined of the children, was given the front tearooms and established the Omotesenke school (*omote* means "front"). Soshitsu, the fourth son, got the back (*ura*) rooms and began Urasenke. All three sons soon went back to work for the feudal lords and prospered in the subsequent years.

page 142: Tea schools all aspire to the same end but differ in style, utensils, emphasis, and methodology. Whole schools of ceramics and other handicrafts developed around these schools as tea masters demanded specific types of designs, shapes, and colors for their tea bowls, kettles, and other paraphernalia. Sometimes the arrangement between the tea family and the potter's family was very cozy indeed, with one having the exclusive right to sell the wares of the other, for a substantial profit. There is a certain tyranny to the *iemoto* system, which may explain why yakuza gangs are

similarly organized. The main advantage to the pyramidal structure becomes readily apparent as you follow the money trail. A beginning tea student pays ¥3,000 (about $21) to his first Urasenke school teacher. From this, the teacher pays Urasenke ¥2,000 for permission to take on a new student. The student then pays the teacher ¥3,000–5,000 a month. At every level of advancement, the student is required to pay another ¥3,000 (¥1,800 to Urasenke/¥1,200 to the teacher). At the next major stage, the student pays ¥4,000 (¥2,500/¥1,500), and this continues over the next three stages. The fee goes up to ¥5,000 (¥3,000/¥2,000) for the next two stages, and then to ¥12,000 (¥7,000/¥5,000). And so on, for a total of a dozen stages over a period of five to six years. At that point, the student can begin studying to become a teacher, paying (in stages again) a total of ¥345,000 (¥245,000/¥100,000). After finishing all this, the student can adopt a new name using the special "tea ideogram" *so-* to indicate his or her status. If the student then wishes to become a full-fledged teacher, it will cost another ¥300,000. The Urasenke organization monitors payments to make sure that teachers do not withhold funds from the organization. It also employs ten full-time calligraphers who spend their day doing nothing but writing out official permission certificates. Currently there are at least 25,000 certified Urasenke teachers, and each has thirty to forty students. Critics say that the rigid hierarchy and training methods stifle individual creativity and innovation in the art. But, in fairness, the schools are something more than just Amway-style cash cows. They function as living museums, where a precious art is nurtured, preserved, and passed on whole to the next generation. The organization also ensures that quality and consistent instruction are available to great masses of ordinary people who might otherwise not be exposed to the national aesthetic. **page 143**: After the Meiji Restoration of 1868 the *iemoto* was officially designated as a "performer," hardly a distinguished title. Urasenke was freer to mass-market tea culture because its rival, Omotesenke, was tied to the powerful Mitsui family and was considered to be the main repository of the tea tradition. Urasenke began the systematic teaching of tea in around 1940 and has been able to grow by revising its methods to keep pace with changing attitudes among modern consumers.

page 144: Because of Kayoko's poor beginnings, her marriage into Urasenke would have been unthinkable had she not been adopted by the relatives of a high-ranking samurai family. She devoted her life to tea and the tea school. She is said to have given money to the police, TV stations, the tax office, and newspapers. In 1943 she gave a large gift to the Japanese army and navy. She also established the custom of having the prime minister and other politicians come to Urasenke for New Year's tea. All her work for the Urasenke name continues to pay off. When a foreign diplomat visits Kyoto, for example, it is Urasenke that he goes to, not Omotesenke or the other tea schools. **page 145**: Samurai warriors in medieval times used to drink tea to help steel themselves before going into battle.

page 146: There are as many as twenty-five industrialists and financiers (the list continues to grow) who belong to Robunkai. Generally the Robunkai group is for people with money, status, or an important name, although some members are actually quite knowledgeable and proficient in the art of tea. The industrialist Konosuke Matsushita was a member before his death. Matsushita contributed considerable amounts to Urasenke. A tea aficionado, Matsushita was not, however, considered much of an expert. **page 147**: Soshitsu has been awarded Brazil's Southern Cross and is an honorary citizen of Boston and an honorary diplomat in Portugal. **page 148**: People pay for Soshitsu's name on a tea bowl, not simply for the snob value but because it increases the worth of the piece by establishing its aesthetic integrity. Soshitsu is, by virtue of his position, one of the leading arbiters of taste in Japan today. Japanese art buyers strike many Western curators and gallery owners as slavish and insecure—they need a major name on the work before they will accept it. The world of traditional arts in Japan is particularly hidebound—a tendency that Urasenke (and almost all other crafts schools) exploit by putting the signature of the master on the piece, whether or not he had anything to do with its actual manufacture. This may help the craftsman, but it may not be especially good for the craft, since it is unlikely that there could be as many outstanding pieces as there are specimens of the *iemoto*'s signature. Soshitsu's signature on a tea bowl can fetch an additional $70,000.

page 149: Urasenke put up a six-story office building in Kyoto in 1980. Floor 1 is a museum, floor 2 is a library of books related to tea, floors 3 and 4 are offices, floor 5 is a training room. Next door are an auditorium and antique teahouses. Many Tankosha art books are related to tea and tea connoisseurship. The company has recently acquired John Weatherhill, a Tokyo-based English-language publisher. Among the hotels that the Tanko Group owns in Hawaii are the Beach Hotel and the Breakers. Tanko is also exclusive agent for the Louvre and the Metropolitan Museum of Art in Japan. There are thirteen overseas branches of Urasenke in cities like Honolulu, Seattle, San Francisco, New York, London, and Paris to serve an estimated 100,000 foreign students of tea. The delicious contradiction that Soshitsu represents as tea aesthete and powerful businessman all in one has made him a favorite target for Japan's scandal magazines, which print rumors about him and sex and money. Soshitsu's carefully nurtured connections with just about every power base in Japan have made him virtually unassailable, however. Many feel that the tea world is in decline, and that there is too much emphasis on the money machine. The story is told of how, in 1802, a feudal lord who was a great lover of tea sent a subordinate to Urasenke in Kyoto to arrange for a tea ceremony. The *iemoto* said that the ceremony would cost fifty silver coins if performed in public and thirty if done privately. "What if I just want to see your tearoom and garden and not have any tea?" the subordinate asked. "In that case," replied the tea master, "only ten silver coins." When the feudal lord heard this story he was greatly disappointed and said, "The spirit of tea has ended in the Sen family."

Toshiro Akibo, David Barich, David Bong, Kenneth M. Butti, Bernie Bullard, Ron Cayo, Shi Yu Chen, Susan Chira, Dan Clark, Richard B. Cohen, Creative Intelligence Associates, Judith Dunham, Lyle Fox, Yoshiharu Fukuhara, Mary Ann Gilderbloom, Harrington-Young Typography and Design, Keiko Hirayama, Hiroko Horiguchi, Lisa Howard, David P. Hughes, Masaki Ide, Yuko Ioki, IPA Company, Jack Jensen, Sam Kawakami, Mari Kida, Fumiko Kitayama, Kitchen, Kazuko Koike, Bill LeBlond, John Lomibao, Daniel Massler, Setsuko Nakamura, Yoko Nakamura, Kanako Nakayama, Masamitsu Ookubo, Hiroshi Oyagi, Pamela Pasti, Ronald D. Pogue, John Roberts, Yoshikuni Sato, Frederik L. Schodt, Mark Schreiber, Tetsuji Shimizu, Shizuko Takano, Mizue Takase, Katsumi Takemori, Susumu Tamaki, Yasuharu Tamiya, Tamiyo Togasaki, Tokyo Pages, Kesao Uchida, Urasenke Foundation, Bill Womack, Stephanie Young, Teruhiko Yumura.